SCHOLASTIC

W9-BMZ-414

Easy

ASSESSMENTS
for Pre-Kindergarten

Laurie B. Fyke

NEW YORK • TORONTO • LONDON • AUCKLAND • SYDNEY
MEXICO CITY • NEW DELHI • HONG KONG • BUENOS AIRES

Teaching *Resources*

Edited by Sarah Longhi and Rebecca Callan
Cover design by Jorge J. Namerow
Interior design by Melinda Belter
Interior illustrations by Maxie Chambliss

ISBN-13 978-0-439-70071-9
ISBN-10 0-439-70071-X

2 3 4 5 6 7 8 9 10   40   16 15 14 13 12 11 10 09 08 07

This book is dedicated to my mom, Vera Geraldine Hamilton,
and to my husband and best friend, James Edward Fyke,
who always provided warmth, support, and encouragement to our family . . .
along with a love of learning.

Special thanks to:
our children, Gregory, Steven, and Susan, for their love and support

*And to the following professionals for the many educational discussions
regarding pre-kindergarten needs and expectations; and for reviewing,
critiquing, and testing the assessment pages:*

Cathie Hamilton, Reading Recovery & Resource Teacher
Jodi Gates, Kindergarten Teacher
Kerrie Sinclair, Kindergarten Teacher
Mary Lynn North, Kindergarten Teacher
Barb Bida, Grade One/Two Teacher
Lynn Orr, Speech Pathologist
Pre-Kindergarten Children

*And the children at Rose Seaton Public School . . .
and Mr. Dante Pirillo, principal, for his support and encouragement.*

Contents

RECORD-KEEPING FORMS

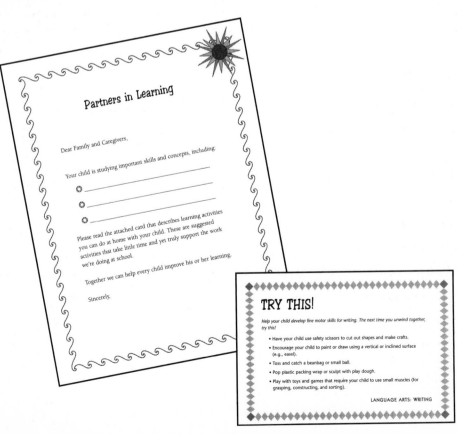

Welcome

As a classroom teacher who enjoyed reading educational books and journals, I became interested in the face and role of assessment—learning to harness what was often an unwieldy process and the ways in which I could best meet my students' needs. With experience, I found that my assessment program benefited from hard-copy observations that I could share with caregivers and also from varied means of determining each child's strengths. After some time, I found that I had developed a practical compilation of assessment tools and resources. This book is the result.

Learning expectations, *standards*, *lesson planning*, *progress reports*: Where to begin? I've included dozens of assessments to help you customize your own assessment toolkit. While the assessments are meaningful, ongoing, and systematic—they constitute a collection, not a program. I've designed them to complement your curriculum and the formal and informal assessment tools and techniques you already use.

As you read this book and think about how you can make the most of the resources provided, I encourage you to keep in mind this observation from Susanne L. Wagner, a research associate with Project Match at Erikson Institute's Herr Research Center.

> *The nature of children's learning is highly integrated, episodic, and nonlinear, so the breadth and depth of their skills and knowledge cannot be fully captured through a point-in-time, content-driven test.*

Capturing all that our ever-changing young learners are beginning to know is a challenge that cannot be met by single measures of achievement, but rather by systematic assessments and anecdotal records throughout the year that track progress in targeted areas. To what end? A holistic, well-rounded picture of how your students have progressed and where you can focus your instructional energies next.

I hope you find all the materials in this book as helpful as I have.

Laurie B. Fyke

(Wagner, Susan L. (2003). *Assessment in the early childhood classroom*. Applied Research in Child Development, Number 4(*1*).

HOW TO USE THIS BOOK

This book is designed to serve as a resource, one that both beginner and seasoned teachers can turn to for help with assessing pre-kindergarten students' progress in language arts and mathematics.

 ## Using Assessment to Inform Instruction

Assessment is most meaningful when the results of it are used to improve children's learning opportunities. You might ask yourself some of the following questions when you think about your assessment program and how it informs your lesson planning: *What systematic, direct, explicit instruction does the class require? What skills or strategies need to be developed in a small-group setting? What is the developmental level of this child? How can I (or a volunteer) support this child's learning?*

To get the big picture of student progress, you'll need to track each child's success with a combination of formal and informal assessment techniques, such as the ones described below. With this well-informed assessment picture, you can account for a variety of factors that might cause a child to perform poorly on a single measure of assessment, such as the child's ability to identify the letters in his or her name or recognize geometric shapes.

OBSERVATION

The primary tool of assessment is observation of children at work and play in the classroom. Each of the reproducible assessment forms provided in this book has a section called Notes, a designated place for recording your observations. There you can record a snapshot of a child's skills at different points in the school year. Or, you can use that section as a place to keep anecdotal records, narrative descriptions of a child's developing skills.

PORTFOLIOS

Collect and date student work throughout the year and file it in a large binder or file folder that can serve as a portfolio. For each child, file the completed assessment forms that you use from this book. Add photocopies or original materials to the portfolio, including: photos of the child engaged in a learning activity, samples of imaginative work (artwork, creative writing), reading-response pages, completed graphic organizers, copies of favorite poems and songs, and titles of favorite books. Plus, you can add work that the child proudly brings from home to share with you

or the class . . . along with pages supplied by a proud family member as a record of his or her child's progress.

Use the portfolios not only to collect work, but also as a place you can go to review a child's progress periodically and offer a snapshot of progress to parents and caregivers. At the end of the school year, send the portfolio home for families to review and share—giving families direct access to a record of the child's needs and strengths as well as another vehicle for supporting and extending learning opportunities over the summer.

PERSONALIZED INSTRUCTION

Children are unique individuals with varying background experiences and knowledge about books, print, oral language, mathematics concepts, social experiences, and the world around them. Therefore, it stands to reason that not all children are ready for the same thing at the same time. In order to support all learners, the curriculum lessons, concepts, skills, and ideas that you present need to be shared in ways that bring into play visual, tactile, and auditory learning modalities. Support children's learning to enable them to feel proud of their accomplishments and to view themselves as successful learners. Teach, reteach, and review lessons to maximize learning opportunities for all children and to consolidate their growing knowledge.

Resources on Appropriate Practices and Assessment

Bodrova, E., Leong, D. J., and Paynter, D. E. (1999) Literacy Standards for Preschool Learners: Redefining Literacy. *Educational Leadership, 57 (2).*

Bredekamp, S. (1987). *Developmentally appropriate practice in early childhood programs serving children birth through age eight.* Washington, DC: National Association for the Education of Young Children.

Mindes, G. (2006). *Assessing young children.* 3rd Edition. Upper Saddle River, NJ. Prentice Hall.

Pokay, P. A. and Tayeh, C. (2000). *256 assessment tips for mathematics teachers.* Upper Saddle River, NJ. Dale Seymour.

Volunteers:

GETTING THE SUPPORT YOU WANT

Having volunteers in the classroom to aid with the assessment process can be enormously helpful and successful . . . if you take time at the start of the school year to establish a clear action plan and develop guidelines for volunteers to follow. Here are some ideas to help you get you started.

Finding the Fit

Conduct an orientation meeting where you help volunteers determine where they fit in with your expectations. To begin, talk about what kinds of skills and behaviors you're looking for in a volunteer. Then ask parents and caregivers to voice their interests, questions, and concerns.

To help volunteers identify how and where they can help in the classroom, invite volunteers to role-play a variety of situations—assisting with one-on-one assessments, guiding small-group instructional activities, monitoring classroom activities, and so on. Some volunteers may find they are comfortable in a variety of helping roles. Others may prefer to volunteer in ways that take them out of the classroom setting, such as photocopying or picking up books at the library.

Training the Team

Volunteers need to be coached and trained to carry out the tasks you require. For example, if you find that you have a volunteer willing to help with one-on-one assessment of children, review the assessment forms with the volunteer. Take time to clearly explain and teach each step of the assessment. Then have the volunteer observe (or shadow) you while you assess several children.

Once you have a team of volunteers in place and assisting with the assessment process, set aside time to evaluate the success of your volunteer program. Invite suggestions from team members, modify your action plan, and retrain volunteers as needed.

Your Assessment Plan

There are many ways you can utilize assessments, but before you begin the process of assessing the students in your classroom, think about your instructional goals. Most likely you will be using your first set of assessments as a baseline to which you'll compare results over the school year. Or, it may be that you plan to examine assessment results to determine individual student strengths or areas that need remediation. Or, perhaps you intend to identify which students would benefit from explicit instruction on a specific skill.

Use the assessment tools in this book to suit your needs. Here are some ideas for keeping your assessment plan organized:

SET UP A SCHEDULE

It follows that you would want to administer baseline assessments at the start of the school year. But when should you do the other assessments? If your school's calendar is divided into quarters, then administer the other three assessments near the close of each quarter. If your school's calendar is divided into semesters or trimesters, then administer the other assessments when you feel the assessments will best capture student progress, but certainly before you complete progress reports. (Make a photocopy of the Assessment Planning Calendar on page 138 to help you organize a schedule.)

GATHER MATERIALS AHEAD OF TIME

Each month, select and photocopy a class set of assessments. Place the assessments that you'll administer in one group and the ones volunteers can administer in another group. (See *Volunteers: Getting the Support You Want* on page 9.) Store each set of assessments inside a sturdy binder or file folder for easy access.

Gather the supplemental materials you need to administer the assessments into a portable container or storage box. (Refer to the materials list at the top of each assessment.) Add to your collection the following: pencils, wax pencils (for writing on laminated pages), a few sheets of blank paper (for masking extraneous print on Student Forms), a photocopy of the Whole Class Profile (for keeping a bird's-eye view on the progress of the entire class), and a class set of photocopied Student Progress Profiles (for recording information about individual student progress). Refer to the record-keeping forms that begin on page 129.

STORE COMPLETED ASSESSMENTS TOGETHER

If you plan to develop student portfolios, you may choose to keep your completed assessment forms in each child's portfolio. (Read more about portfolios on page 7.) If you plan to keep all of your completed assessment forms together in one place, keep them in a large binder and organize them by student, using section dividers.

How to Administer the Assessments

FAMILIARIZE YOURSELF WITH THE TOOL

It can be weeks between when you've selected an assessment to administer and the time your schedule actually permits you to administer it. Take time before you begin to administer an assessment to review the procedures you'll need to follow and to make sure you have all the materials you'll need.

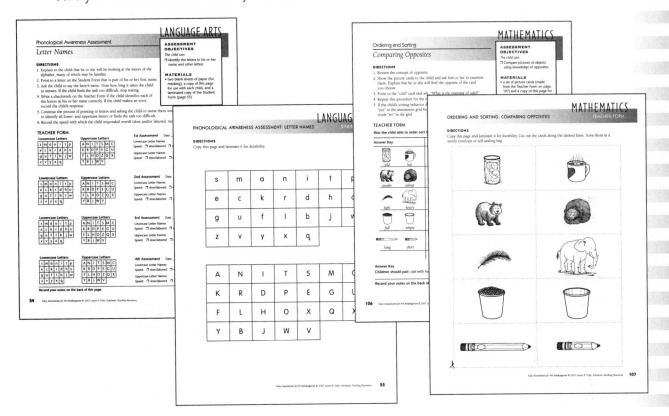

CONSIDER THE SETTING

Designate a space in the classroom as an assessment station, a place where children can readily focus on the tasks you'll ask of them. For example, you may not want your workspace to be beside a window if it faces the playground. Once you've found a space that will work well, arrange chairs around a table or desk so that a child can sit facing forward in front of you and close enough to hear you easily.

You may find it helpful to enlist volunteers in your assessment program. (See *Volunteers: Getting the Support You Want* on page 9.) Or, if you prefer to administer the assessments yourself, consider administering some assessments in small-group settings.

WRITE THE NAME AND DATE

Before you begin explaining the tasks you want the child to do, write the child's name and the date on the assessment forms. That's information you'll need for the rest of the school year.

PUT IN PLAIN WORDS WHAT IS EXPECTED

Explain the directions on the assessment form as the child needs to hear them. That way, the child isn't inundated with multi-step instructions, but rather can proceed with following just one task at a time.

RECORD THE RESULTS

After you administer an assessment, record the child's performance in the Teacher Form section of the assessment sheet. For some assessments, the form will prompt you to record the child's performance by tallying the number of questions answered correctly and recording the results on a grid. For other assessments, the form will prompt you to record whether the child's behavior demonstrates understanding of the skills being addressed. Most forms include a Notes section, a place where you can record further details about a child's performance. For information about deciphering the scores and using your observations in a diagnostic capacity, read Interpret the Scores below.

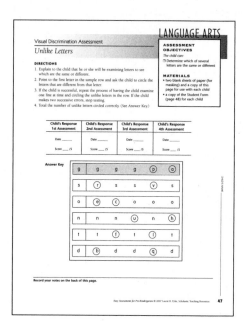

INTERPRET THE SCORES

As you read a score, think about when you administered the assessment and how it relates to the child's learning progress over time. For instance, a score of 0/10 at the first assessment isn't reason to panic. It is just a baseline assessment that provides you with information about what skills a child may have mastered already and what skills he or she may need to gain knowledge of through your instruction.

Resist the temptation to label scores with the letter designations of A, B, C, D, F. Instead, ask yourself what each score might mean in terms of giving individualized instruction, providing for additional services, and lesson planning. You may find it helpful to look at scores as points along a continuum with N (skills not apparent), B (beginning to develop), D (developing), P (present), and E (exceeding age expectations).

How to Calculate Percentages

Take the numerator (the tally) and divide it by the denominator. (e.g., A score of 6/8 indicates .75 or 75 percent.)

- Empower children by guiding them toward independence. We are in a helping profession and often over-assist the young reader. Independent readers need to assume ownership of the learning process. Provide text with words the reader can decode, text based on his or her knowledge of sounds that have been taught. Let the child turn the pages, point to the text, and blend sounds. Avoid depending on picture clues, a practice that can lead to over-guessing.

- Help children learn essential language skills and strategies by providing direct, explicit systematic instruction . . . and by thinking aloud, modeling, and drawing on numerous and varied songs, games, and learning activities.

- Provide young children with frequent and diverse opportunities to work with oral language. Engaging activities like singing songs and playing games facilitate the decoding process in both reading and writing. I recommend using a synthetic phonics program that includes songs and kinesthetic actions for each phoneme.

ADDITIONAL SUPPORT MATERIALS

CONNECTIONS TO THE STANDARDS

As you plan instruction and assessment, keep in mind your school district's and state's standards and the recommendations of professional organizations and research communities.

For a quick reference regarding the Mid-continent Research for Education and Learning (McREL) guidelines for reading and writing, refer to page 23. To learn more about the skills addressed in the National Council of Teachers of Mathematics (NCTM) standards for pre-kindergarten, turn to page 83.

Assessment Category	Page	Assessment Tool Title	Number and Operations	Algebra	Geometry	Measurement	Data Analysis and Probability	Problem Solving	Reasoning and Proof	Communication	Connections	Representation
SHAPES	91	Properties and Relationships			✓			✓	✓	✓	✓	✓
NUMERATION	93	Recognizing Numerals	✓									✓
	96	Quantity and Correspondence	✓					✓			✓	✓
	98	Comparing Sets by Number	✓				✓	✓	✓	✓	✓	✓
ORDERING & SORTING	100	Comparing Sets by Attributes	✓		✓	✓		✓	✓	✓		
	102	Smallest to Largest		✓		✓		✓	✓	✓	✓	✓
	104	Three Stages of Development		✓		✓		✓	✓	✓	✓	✓
	106	Comparing Opposites		✓		✓		✓	✓	✓	✓	✓
	108	Simple Patterns		✓		✓		✓	✓	✓	✓	✓
MEASUREMENT, TIME, & MONEY	111	Comparing Length, Weight, and Capacity				✓		✓	✓	✓	✓	✓
	113	Matching Tools and Traits				✓		✓	✓	✓	✓	✓
	115	Using Time Vocabulary	✓			✓		✓	✓	✓	✓	✓
	117	Matching Coins	✓			✓		✓	✓	✓	✓	✓
SPATIAL RELATIONSHIPS & TERMINOLOGY	119	Relative Positions			✓	✓		✓	✓	✓	✓	✓
OPERATION & PLACE VALUE	121	Math Stories	✓			✓		✓	✓	✓	✓	✓
	124	Dictated Math Stories	✓	✓		✓		✓	✓	✓	✓	✓
CHARTS & GRAPHS	126	Collecting and Analyzing Data	✓			✓	✓	✓	✓	✓	✓	✓

EXPECTATIONS/TIME LINE GRIDS

Read How to Use the Expectations/Time Line Grids (page 18) for guidance about making the most of the language arts and mathematics grids in this book. Ready to use the grids as quick references? Turn to the language arts grid (page 26) or the mathematics grid (page 84).

WHAT-ELSE-KIDS-NEED-TO-KNOW CHECKLISTS

These checklists (pages 30 and 88) complement the lists of learning expectations on the grids. They provide you with the information you can use to strengthen and assess skills not addressed by the assessments in this book.

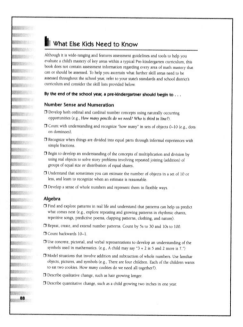

RECORD-KEEPING FORMS

Reproducible record-keeping forms have been provided to help you manage important information, save time, and stay organized.

Student Progress Profile: Photocopy class sets of the Student Progress Profile forms for language arts (page130) and mathematics (page 131). Use these forms to consolidate and record data regarding individual student performance on assessments.

Whole Class Profile: Make one copy of the language arts form (pages 132 and 133) and one copy of the mathematics form (pages 134 and 135). Record assessment results and then step back. You can look at the entire class's performance on a particular assessment or within a particular skill set . . . at a glance.

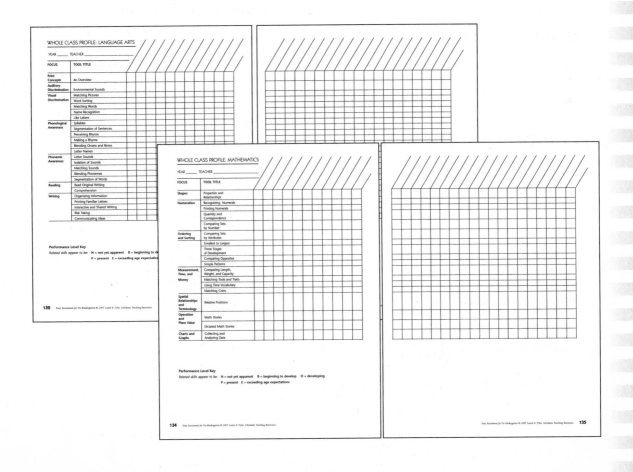

Make-Your-Own Profiles: Customize your own Student Progress Profiles and Whole Class Profiles with the blank reproducible templates provided on pages 136 and 137.

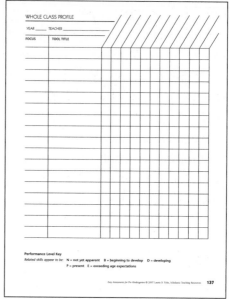

Assessment Planning Calendar: Use the reproducible calendar on page 138 to set up an assessment schedule that covers the whole year. For a list of the language arts assessments in this book, turn to page 35. For mathematics, refer to the assessments grid on page 83, Connections to the Math Standards.

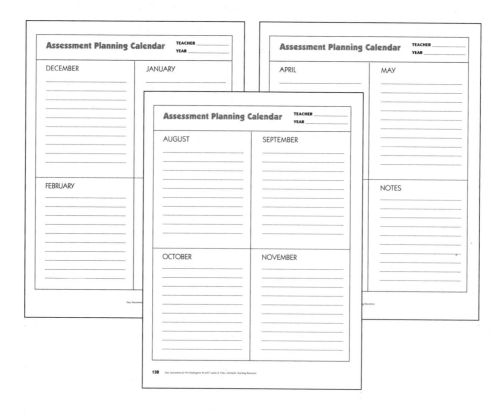

SEND-HOME CARDS

Each learning card contains step-by-step instructions for an activity that may be completed at home. Just photocopy the learning card that addresses the skills you want a particular child to practice. (The cards begin on page 146.) Then photocopy the appropriate seasonal companion letter (letters begin on page 142) that explains to the child's family or caregiver that the learning activity described on the card will give the student needed practice on a targeted skill. Be sure to personalize the letter and send it (along with the card) home with the child.

The learning cards can also be useful for volunteers who might use the cards to work with small groups of children on a key skill. You may also find that the learning cards are a source of ideas you can turn to during lesson planning.

EARLY YEARS ARE LEARNING YEARS™

The reproducible articles included in this book provide tips on a variety of topics and can be used to introduce teaching ideas and practices to families, caregivers, and classroom volunteers. Here are a couple of ways you might use them:

- At the start of the school year, send home a copy of Your Child's First Report Card (pages 162 and 163) with each student. Reading the article will help families learn ways to monitor and advance their child's progress.

- When you send correspondence to families, consider including one of the articles—Raising a Reader (pages 164 and 165), Mathematics Through Play (pages 166 and 167), or Singing as a Teaching Tool (pages 168 and 169). Each article provides valuable information about supporting children's learning.

How to Use the Expectations/Time Line Grids

Use the information in the language arts and mathematics grids (pages 26 and 84) to help inform your lesson planning and instruction—and as a resource you can turn to as you address the specific needs of all of your students. To put a few of the most fundamental aspects of teaching at your fingertips, each grid is divided into three categories: Learning Expectations, Scope and Sequence Guidelines, and Evaluation and Support.

LEARNING EXPECTATIONS represent the skills and strategies a pre-kindergartner is expected to master over the course of a school year. The academic skills listed are intended as benchmarks specifically for most children age 4 to 6 years.

Note that each child comes to school at a developmental level consistent with his or her unique personal, academic, and social base. You may find that one child may master the skills outlined in the grid, while another will continue to develop and extend his or her learning.

LANGUAGE ARTS LEARNING EXPECTATIONS *By the end of the school year, a pre-kindergartner should begin to . . .*	Scope and Sequence Guidelines Time Line (Spanning Ten Months)			
	1	2	3	4
PRINT CONCEPTS				
Demonstrate knowledge of book orientation.	X	X	X	
Understand that books have titles, authors, and often illustrations	X	X	X	X
Develop predictions.				
Demonstrate knowledge that print carries meaning.		X	X	X
Demonstrate knowledge of left-to-right and top-to-bottom directionality.		X	X	X
Demonstrate knowledge of word-by-word matching and left-to-right movement across the page.				
Demonstrate knowledge of movement to the next page.		X	X	X
Discriminate between letter and word.				
Recognize that words are separated by spaces.				X
Demonstrate understanding of text layout.				X
AUDITORY DISCRIMINATION				
Identify environmental sounds.	X	X	X	X
VISUAL DISCRIMINATION				
Discriminate between pictures that are the same or different.	X	X	X	
Sort words by visual cues.				X
Discriminate between words that are the same or different.				X
Identify his or her first name among three unfamiliar names.	X	X	X	X
Identify his or her first name among five classmates' names.		X	X	X
Determine which of several letters are the same or different.				X

SCOPE AND SEQUENCE GUIDELINES are provided to help you with the nuts and bolts of planning and instruction. After all, determining which skills and strategies to focus instruction on can be a challenge. Determining when to teach those skills and strategies (from a developmental perspective) can be even more challenging.

Think of the guidelines as just that, guidelines that are set over a ten-month school year. Use them to help you reflect on the learning happening in your classroom and as a support as you observe children for mastery of skills.

EVALUATION AND SUPPORT page references are included to make navigating the reproducible materials in this book easier. If you need to evaluate a student's progress, look for the skill in the Learning Expectations column and read across the row to the Evaluation and Support column. There you will find a page listing for an assessment tool you can photocopy and use in the classroom. And if you need to provide additional support for a student, there's a reproducible Partners-in-Learning Letter for families and Send-Home Cards you can photocopy and send home for extra practice. For more information about working with families as partners in teaching, see page 17.

Scope and Sequence Guidelines						Evaluation and Support	
Time Line (Spanning Ten Months)						Assessment Tool Page	Send-Home Card Page
5	6	7	8	9	10		
						36	146
X						36	146
X	X	X	X	X	X	36	146
X	X	X	X	X	X	36	146
X	X	X	X	X	X	36	146
X	X	X	X	X	X	36	146
X	X	X				36	146
X	X	X	X	X	X	36	146
X	X	X	X	X	X	36	146
X	X	X	X	X	X	36	146
X						37	146, 147
						39	147
X	X	X	X	X	X	41	147
X	X	X	X	X	X	43	148
						45	
X	X	X	X			45	
X	X	X	X	X	X	47	147

Language Arts

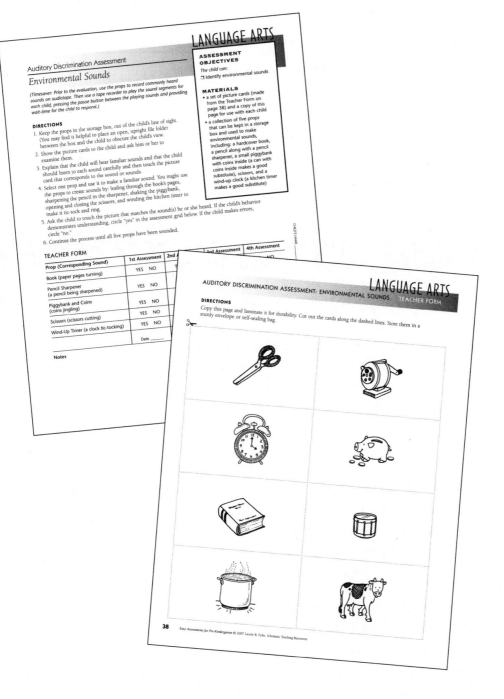

Auditory Discrimination Assessment

Environmental Sounds

(Timesaver: Prior to the evaluation, use the props to record commonly heard sounds on audiotape. Then use a tape recorder to play the sound segments for each child, pressing the pause button between the playing sounds and providing wait-time for the child to respond.)

DIRECTIONS

1. Keep the props in the storage box, out of the child's line of sight. (You may find it helpful to place an open, upright file folder between the box and the child to obscure the child's view.)
2. Show the picture cards to the child and ask him or her to examine them.
3. Explain that the child will hear familiar sounds and that the child should listen to each sound carefully and then touch the picture card that corresponds to the sound or sounds.
4. Select one prop and use it to make a familiar sound. You might use the props to create sounds by: leafing through the book's pages, sharpening the pencil in the sharpener, shaking the piggybank, opening and closing the scissors, and winding the kitchen timer to make it tic-tock and ring.
5. Ask the child to touch the picture that matches the sound(s) he or she heard. If the child's behavior demonstrates understanding, circle "yes" in the assessment grid below. If the child makes errors, circle "no."
6. Continue the process until all five props have been sounded.

TEACHER FORM

Prop (Corresponding Sound)	1st Assessment	2nd A	3rd Assessment	4th Assessment
Book (paper pages turning)	YES NO	Y		NO
Pencil Sharpener (a pencil being sharpened)	YES NO			
Piggybank and Coins (coins jingling)	YES NO			
Scissors (scissors cutting)	YES NO			
Wind-Up Timer (a clock tic-tocking)	YES NO			

Date _____

Notes

LANGUAGE ARTS

ASSESSMENT OBJECTIVES

The child can:
☐ Identify environmental sounds

MATERIALS

- a set of picture cards (made from the Teacher Form on page 38) and a copy of this page for use with each child
- a collection of five props that can be kept in a storage box and used to make environmental sounds, including: a hardcover book, a pencil along with a pencil sharpener, a small piggybank with coins inside (a can with coins inside makes a good substitute), scissors, and a wind-up clock (a kitchen timer makes a good substitute)

AUDITORY DISCRIMINATION ASSESSMENT: ENVIRONMENTAL SOUNDS

LANGUAGE ARTS
TEACHER FORM

DIRECTIONS

Copy this page and laminate it for durability. Cut out the cards along the dashed lines. Store them in a sturdy envelope or self-sealing bag.

Introduction to Language Arts

Use the resources and materials noted below to help you support all learners and evaluate learning in the following areas: print concepts, auditory discrimination, visual discrimination, phonological awareness, phonemic awareness, reading, and writing.

- Resources for Helping Struggling Readers and Writers, below
- How to Use the Expectations/Time Line Grids, page 18
- Connections to the Language Arts Standards, page 23
- Continuum of Writing Stages, page 23
- Expectations/Time Line Grid, page 26
- What Else Kids Need to Know, page 30
- Important Terms About Teaching and Learning Language Arts, page 31
- A List of the Assessments: Language Arts, page 35

Resources for Helping Struggling Readers and Writers

Tap these sources for guidance on evaluating and supporting all learners:

NATIONAL CENTER FOR LEARNING DISABILITIES (NCLD)
Through research, public awareness programs, and grants, the NCLD serves to educate and support children, families, and professionals. By visiting the Web site at www.ncld.org, you can access LD Talk, which provides an on-line chat with experts in the field.

WEPMAN'S AUDITORY DISCRIMINATION TEST (ADT)
Created in 1958 by Joseph M. Wepman, Ph.D. in an effort to help detect auditory discrimination problems in young children. The second edition is available for purchase through Western Psychological Services, 12031 Wilshire Boulevard, Los Angeles, CA 90025, (800) 648-8857. Visit www.wpspublish.com or e-mail customer service at customerservice@wpspublish.com.

TEST OF AUDITORY ANALYSIS (TAAS)
This test can assist with identifying young children who need help with word analysis skills. Copies of this test developed by Jerome Rosner are available for purchase through the distributor: Academic Therapy Publications, 20 Commercial Blvd, Novato, CA 94949, (800) 422-7249. Or, visit the web site at AcademicTherapy.com.

CONNECTIONS TO THE LANGUAGE ARTS STANDARDS

Mid-Continent Research for Education and Learning (McREL), a nationally recognized, nonprofit organization, has compiled and evaluated state standards and recommendations from professional organizations—and proposed what teachers should provide for their students to become proficient in language arts, among other curriculum areas. To learn how the reading and writing assessments in this book support these standards for pre-kindergarten, visit the Web site: http://mcrel.org. For additional information about McREL and to learn more about the topics and benchmarks within each standard, read *Content Knowledge: A Compendium of Standards and Benchmarks for K–12 Education*. Mid-Continent Research for Education and Learning, 2006. This fourth edition of the compendium provides benchmarks within each standard that are tailored for pre-kindergarten, taking into account developmentally appropriate content and practice.

CONTINUUM OF WRITING STAGES

Children's written communication skills grow more sophisticated in association with the development of motor control, pincer grip, language skills, and knowledge of letter formation. Examining informative scribble trails, drawings, and letter-like forms can give us insights to a child's literacy growth and instructional needs.

Use the illustration at the right as a guide for observing and assessing pencil positioning and grip. (You might also take into consideration the proper use of body mechanics, paper positioning, and ergonomic pencil-grip devices.)

Refer to the writing samples below and the descriptions that accompany them as a point of reference while you evaluate each child's current stage of writing development.

Scribble/Picture Writing

SCRIBBLE/PICTURE WRITING

A child may . . .

- explore the empty space of a sheet of paper.
- use pictures to represent words or letters. (See Children's Drawings as Indicators on page 25.)

LINEAR SCRIBBLE WRITING

A child may . . .

- draw squiggles and other shapes to represent letters.
- write forms that look like letters.

DRAWING AND SCRIBBLING

A child may . . .

- write random forms that look like letters.
- use letters in word-like groupings, but there may be little relationship between the letters and sounds in the words written.

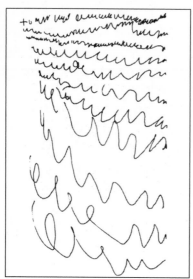

Linear Scribble Writing

Drawing and Scribbling Stage

Early Phonemic Writing

Transitional Writing

EARLY PHONEMIC WRITING

A child may . . .

- make use of rebus writing (with letters and pictures).
- use some letters to stand for sounds in words.
- form some letters correctly.

TRANSITIONAL WRITING

A child may . . .

- use a top-to-bottom arrangement for writing.
- form most letters correctly.
- show a mixture of conventional and phonetic spellings.
- write some readable words.
- compose some sentences.

CONVENTIONAL WRITING

A child may . . .

- write readable words and sentences.
- form most letters correctly.
- spell most words correctly.
- use some punctuation.

Adapted from "Developing Literacy: A Whole-Child View,"
a Scholastic Literacy Research Paper by D. R. Reutzel.

Children's Drawings as Indicators

As you observe young children's drawings, take into consideration students' developing abilities across a variety of domains. Artwork will range from scribbles to representational and simple to complex. Here is some guidance in terms of what to look for by the end of pre-kindergarten:

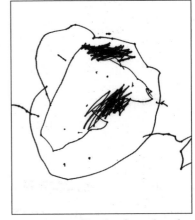

extension of limbs from head

extension of limbs from body

addition of details

A drawing may contain . . .
- A closed shape or form
- A figure drawing (e.g., a circle-shaped head with lines extending from it)
- Some recognizable features (e.g., eyes, mouth)

A drawing may even show evidence of . . .
- Arrangement of space (e.g., ground, sky)
- More precise positioning of elements (e.g., facial features, limbs)
- Inclusion of details (e.g., clothing, eyelashes)

addition of landscape

LANGUAGE ARTS LEARNING EXPECTATIONS

By the end of the school year, a pre-kindergartner should begin to . . .

Scope and Sequence Guidelines

Time Line (Spanning Ten Months)

	1	2	3	4
PRINT CONCEPTS				
Demonstrate knowledge of book orientation.	X	X	X	
Understand that books have titles, authors, and often illustrations	X	X	X	X
Develop predictions.				
Demonstrate knowledge that print carries meaning.		X	X	X
Demonstrate knowledge of left-to-right and top-to-bottom directionality.		X	X	X
Demonstrate knowledge of word-by-word matching and left-to-right movement across the page.				
Demonstrate knowledge of movement to the next page.		X	X	X
Discriminate between letter and word.				
Recognize that words are separated by spaces.				X
Demonstrate understanding of text layout.				X
AUDITORY DISCRIMINATION				
Identify environmental sounds.	X	X	X	X
VISUAL DISCRIMINATION				
Discriminate between pictures that are the same or different.	X	X	X	
Sort words by visual cues.				X
Discriminate between words that are the same or different.				X
Identify his or her first name among three unfamiliar names.	X	X	X	X
Identify his or her first name among five classmates' names.		X	X	X
Determine which of several letters are the same or different.				X
PHONOLOGICAL AWARENESS				
Clap and count the number of syllables in a given word.	X	X	X	X
Segment sentences into words.	X	X	X	X
Identify a rhyme.	X	X	X	X
Produce rhyming words.	X	X	X	X
Blend onsets and rimes.		X	X	X
Identify the letters in his or her name and other letters.				
PHONEMIC AWARENESS				
Recognize and say the sound of letters in his or her name and other letters.	X	X	X	X
Identify the beginning and ending sound of words.	X	X	X	X
Match words that begin or end with the same sound.		X	X	X
Blend phonemes together to say VC, CV, CVC, and CCVC words.	X	X	X	X
Segment words into phonemes.	X	X	X	X

Scope and Sequence Guidelines Time Line (Spanning Ten Months)						Evaluation and Support	
						Assessment Tool Page	Send-Home Card Page
5	6	7	8	9	10		
						36	146
X						36	146
X	X	X	X	X	X	36	146
X	X	X	X	X	X	36	146
X	X	X	X	X	X	36	146
X	X	X	X	X	X	36	146
X	X	X				36	146
X	X	X	X	X	X	36	146
X	X	X	X	X	X	36	146
X	X	X	X	X	X	36	146
X						37	146, 147
						39	147
X	X	X	X	X	X	41	147
X	X	X	X	X	X	43	148
						45	
X	X	X	X			45	
X	X	X	X	X	X	47	147
X	X	X	X			49	148
X	X	X	X	X	X	50	148
X	X	X				51	148, 151
X	X	X	X	X	X	52	148, 151
X	X	X	X	X	X	53	149
X	X	X	X	X	X	54	152
X	X	X	X	X	X	56	152
X	X	X	X	X	X	59	150
X	X	X				60	150
X	X	X	X	X	X	62	152
X	X	X	X	X	X	63	150

LANGUAGE ARTS LEARNING EXPECTATIONS

By the end of the school year, a pre-kindergartner should begin to . . .

	Scope and Sequence Guidelines Time Line (Spanning Ten Months)			
	1	2	3	4
READING				
Use emergent reading skills to read his or her original writing.				
Read simple CVC words.				
Understand that writing includes pictures, letters, and words to communicate information and meaning.		X	X	X
Use listening skills to comprehend a sentence.				
WRITING				
Draw a self-portrait.	X	X	X	X
Demonstrate organizational skills using arrangement of picture details, text, and position on page.		X	X	X
Demonstrate an established hand preference.	X	X	X	X
Demonstrate a correct pencil grip.	X	X	X	X
Print his or her name legibly.	X	X	X	X
Use knowledge of letters to write or copy letters or words legibly.	X	X	X	X
Use phonic knowledge to spell simple words.				
Contribute ideas during an interactive writing activity.			X	X
Express ideas by describing pictures, dictating, drawing, or storytelling.	X	X	X	X
Use emergent forms of writing for a variety of purposes.	X	X	X	X
Write using an assortment of tools and materials.	X	X	X	X
Perform emergent writing in a variety of formats.				
Perform emergent writing in a variety of genres.				

Scope and Sequence Guidelines						Evaluation and Support	
Time Line (Spanning Ten Months)						Assessment Tool Page	Send-Home Card Page
5	6	7	8	9	10		
		X	X	X	X	64	
X	X	X	X	X	X	64	
X	X	X	X	X	X	64	
		X	X	X	X	66	151, 152
X	X	X	X	X	X	68	
X	X	X	X	X	X	68	
X	X	X	X	X	X	68	153
X	X	X	X	X	X	68	153
X						70	
X	X	X	X	X	X	70	153
X	X	X	X	X	X	70	150
X	X	X	X	X	X	72	
X	X	X	X	X	X	74	153
X	X	X	X	X	X	74	
X	X	X	X	X	X	74	
			X	X	X	76	
			X	X	X	76	

What Else Kids Need to Know

Teaching basic reading and writing skills in creative and engaging ways is a challenge, a challenge compounded by the reality that there are so many important skills that children need to know. The assessment guidelines and tools in this book will help you assess a child's mastery in several essential areas within a typical pre-kindergarten curriculum. To help you determine what further language arts skills need to be assessed throughout the school year, refer to your state's standards and school district's curriculum and consider the lists provided below.

By the end of the school year, a pre-kindergartner should begin to . . .

Oral Communication

❏ Recite short poems and songs.

❏ Share reflections, thoughts, information, and ideas.

❏ Connect new information to prior knowledge and personal experiences.

❏ Communicate emotions and needs to peers and adults.

❏ Speak audibly in complete, coherent sentences.

❏ Describe simple one- and two-step directions.

❏ Follow simple one- and two-step directions and respond appropriately to familiar questions.

❏ Participate in class discussions, oral activities, and dramatizations.

❏ Respond to literature and life events by asking questions, expressing feelings, relating to personal experiences, and sharing ideas.

❏ Demonstrate enjoyment and increased understanding of language by joining in when a teacher reads repeated parts of a story, leaves out a predictable word in a story, asks for echo reading, or makes up new songs and chants.

❏ Listen and respond to others by paying attention to a speaker, enjoying a story, taking turns speaking within a group setting, and staying on topic.

❏ Use expression and gestures to communicate more effectively.

❏ Draw on specialized vocabulary related to mathematics, science, and the world around them.

Reading Comprehension

❏ Demonstrate an understanding of story by using picture clues, prior knowledge, and context to make predictions and inferences about story content.

❏ Distinguish between reality and fantasy, fiction and non-fiction.

❑ Retell events, familiar stories, or favorite books. Refer to details, characters, and sequence.

❑ Relate information from non-fiction material that has been read aloud. Or, describe how a story connects to what he or she knows already.

❑ Reflect on connections between personal experiences and those of storybook characters.

❑ Ask and answer questions about the story's literary elements.

❑ Complete simple graphic organizers with a teacher.

Understanding Non-Print Resources

❑ Identify and discuss various types of media.

❑ Respond to media by means of discussion, art, music, and creative movement.

IMPORTANT TERMS ABOUT TEACHING AND LEARNING LANGUAGE ARTS

ALPHABETIC PRINCIPLE   The concept that oral language can be recorded in print, print can be converted into speech, and alphabet letters represent sounds in languages such as English. (See *analytic phonics, phonics,* and *synthetic phonics.*)

ANALOGY   The ability to manipulate and think about words and the way words are formed. In making an analogy, a reader makes connections between what he knows and what he is trying to figure out.

Analogy is also a strategy used by developed readers, who—with their extended vocabulary and ability to make reading or writing connections—divide a word's onset and rime, recall word patterns, and automatically transfer this knowledge. (e.g., To read the word *sprout*, a child makes connections between *spr-* [the onset he recognizes from the word *spring*] and the word *out*.)

ANALYTIC PHONICS   An instructional method in which readers move from looking at the whole word to looking at the sounds and symbols within the word, identifying spelling patterns and word meanings. Analytic phonics promotes a child's understanding of the concept of words, builds automaticity in word recognition, and provides regular opportunities for readers to compare and categorize words.

AUDITORY DISCRIMINATION   A skill that begins with identifying similarities and differences between environmental sounds (e.g., whistle, bell, animal sounds). After fine-tuning the ears, a child can detect similarities and differences between words (e.g., leash, lease) and eventually the sounds in language (e.g., For English: /b/ and /p/, /m/ and /n/).

AUTOMATICITY   The ability to quickly and accurately process information with limited attention or effort applied to the task (e.g., math facts, reading, writing, and spelling). Reading or mathematical fluency is increased by the *automaticity* of the response.

BLEND   Two or more adjacent consonant sounds that form a *blended sound* while retaining the sound of each individual letter (e.g., *sl* -ip , be -*lt*, *spl* -ash).

BLENDING   The ability to combine individual speech sounds (phonemes) together to read a word (e.g., /r/-/ai/-/n/ rain). (See *irregular word*.)

COMPREHENSION   The ability to understand and make sense of text. Readers combine oral language skills and decoding fluency with personal experience and background knowledge in order to draw meaning from printed text.

CONCEPTS OF PRINT   An observational survey used to determine what readers are attending to when they look at books (e.g., book orientation, directionality, features of print).

ELISION   A method that involves omitting one or more sounds in a word— syllable(s), consonant(s), or vowel(s). By drawing on this central auditory skill, elision tasks require a child to recognize small differences between syllables and phonemes. This method can help identify hearing and speech deficits. Elision tasks are considered highly predictive phonemic awareness tasks as they are useful in assessing how well a child understands speech and can manipulate phonemes within the spoken word.

FLUENCY   A skill that, when referred to within the context of reading, draws on a child's automatic recall of the sound and symbol(s) represented. Strengthening a child's ability to navigate digraphs and alternate spellings increases word recognition, accuracy, speed, and, in turn, fluency. Among the strategies that can help develop students' fluency skills are oral reading, rereading decodable text, and listening to modeled reading. (See *automaticity* and *word recognition*.)

GRAPHEME   A symbol, alphabet letter, or combination of alphabet letters within a language's writing system that represents a single speech sound. In the English language more that one grapheme may represent a single phoneme (e.g., /ē/: *meet*; /ī/: *night*). (See *phoneme*.)

IRREGULAR WORD   A word with a spelling pattern that cannot be sounded out easily by means of blending the regular sounds of the word (e.g., *was, me, one, said, come, does*).

METACOGNITION   A process by which one reflects on how he or she learns effectively and then modifies patterns of behavior accordingly.

ONSET   The initial consonant or consonant cluster that precedes the first vowel in a word (e.g., *c* -at, *pl* -ay, *str* -ing) except *qu-*. (See *rime*.)

PHONEME   Refers to the smallest unit in a spoken word and an individual letter's sound. There are roughly 44 phonemes in the English language. A phoneme is represented in print with backslashes / / marking each sound used in oral language (e.g., *at* = /a/ /t/; *pin* = /p/ /i/ /n/; *shop* = /sh/ /o/ /p/).

PHONEMIC AWARENESS   A skill that involves differentiating sounds in oral language. A developing reader learns to focus on and manipulate the individual sounds (phonemes) in spoken words. To build phonemic awareness skills, direct, explicit instruction might include:
- naming and recognizing beginning, ending, and middle sounds
- blending sounds to prepare for reading words (e.g., /m/ /a/ /n/ to form *man*)
- segmenting sounds (e.g., *sat*—/s/ /a/ /t/)
- isolating, deleting, adding, and substituting sounds

PHONICS   A system of instruction based on the principle that children can connect speech sounds (phonemes) to alphabet letters in order to form words. Through direct, explicit, systematic instruction children learn to understand that . . .
- as letters vary from word to word, so do sounds
- one speech sound may have several different spellings (e.g., *play*, *raid*, *cake*)
- some letters of the alphabet have more than one sound (e.g., /s/c—*city*, /k/c—*cat*)
- two letters may make one speech sound (e.g., *that*, *chair*)
- some letter(s) may be used for specific beginning, middle, or ending sounds
- it is possible to segment words in order to match each sound (phoneme) heard in the word with alphabet letters
- a writer can use both phonetic and conventional spelling to record his or her thoughts in print

(See *alphabetic principle*, *analytic phonics*, and *synthetic phonics*.)

PHONOLOGICAL AWARENESS   Refers to one's ability to identify and manipulate spoken language. To build phonological awareness skills, direct, explicit instruction might include:
- discriminating between spoken words
- recognizing that sentences are made up of words
- distinguishing and generating rhyming words
- identifying the number of syllables in a word
- blending the onset and rime
- omitting parts of a word (e.g., initial sounds: *s*-ap, *s*-lap)
- substituting the onset to make new words (e.g., *sl*-eep; *b*-eep; *sh*-eep)
- using the phonemic awareness skills of blending and segmentation
- connecting letter sounds with printed letters

RHYMING   The repetition of two or more similar-ending sounds in words (e.g., *write*, *right*, *light*; *rode*, *road*, *toad*).

RIME   The vowel and remaining phonemes that follow the onset of a word (e.g., d *-og*, sl *-ide*, spl *-endid*). Word families share the same *rime* unit (e.g., *pat*, *cat*, *that*, *splat*). (See *onset*.)

SEGMENTING   Refers to a reader's ability to divide a spoken or printed word, pausing between the word parts. Segmenting may be performed at the phoneme level and the word level (e.g., compound words, onset, and rime).

   Segmenting skills may be applied to help spell a word—a task that involves separating individual speech sounds (phonemes) and identifying alternate spellings of digraphs, as applicable (e.g., *pan* /p/-/a/-/n/; *pie* /p/-/ie/; *right* /r/-/igh/-/t/). Likewise, a reader may draw on segmenting skills in order to hear a sound within a word and identify the sound's relative position (e.g., beginning, middle, end).

SIGHT WORD   A word composed of graphemes that have not yet been addressed by direct instruction, but that is predictable based on its context.

SYLLABLE   A unit of pronunciation that contains a vowel.

SYNTHETIC PHONICS   An instructional method that emphasizes teaching letter sounds in isolation, synthesizing (blending letter sounds to read a word), and segmenting (separating letter sounds to print a word). Synthetic phonics promotes the understanding and use of the alphabetic principle by increasing letter recognition skills and strengthening the sound/symbol connection.

VISUAL DISCRIMINATION   The ability to distinguish one object from another, pair words that are the same or different, and differentiate letter shapes.

VOCABULARY DEVELOPMENT   Refers to a reader's acquisition of terminology, expressions, and technical terms. Vocabulary growth assists a reader's overall language development, including improving comprehension of printed text and expressive story writing skills.

WORD RECOGNITION   The ability to read familiar, decodable, and irregular words both quickly and effortlessly.

A List of the Assessments: Language Arts

Print Concepts Assessment

An Overview

ASSESSMENT OBJECTIVES

Behaviors or understandings to look for:
See Teacher Form below.

MATERIALS
• a few books (see Step 1 for guidance) and a copy of this page for use with each child

DIRECTIONS

1. Collect a few books you think may be unfamiliar to the children. Each book should contain at least one page with only one line of text and another page with at least two lines of text.

2. Work with the child you're assessing to select a book that is unfamiliar to him or her. You might say: *Do you know this book? Have you read this story?*

3. Explain that you will be asking the child some questions about the book that you believe he or she can answer. Then say prompts similar to those suggested below.

4. If the child responds correctly, record a checkmark beside the assessment objective. If the child makes an error, record the error along with your observations on the back of the page.

TEACHER FORM

Suggested Prompts	What behaviors or understandings to look for.	Assessment			
		1st	2nd	3rd	4th
Show me the front cover of this book. Show me the back of this book.	knowledge of book orientation				
Show me the title of this book Point to where you think the author's name is printed.	recognizes that books have titles, authors, and often illustrators				
Read the title and ask, What do you think this story is about?	develops predictions				
Show me the page where the story starts.	knowledge that print carries meaning				
Point to the first word on this page. (Use page with two lines of text.)	knowledge of left-to-right and top-to-bottom directionality				
Pretend you are reading this book. Use your finger to follow the words. (Use page with two lines of text.)	knowledge of word-by-word matching and left-to-right movement across the page				
Where would you read next?	knowledge of movement to the next page				
Pretend you are reading this book. Use your finger to follow the words. (Use page with two lines of text.)	knowledge of left-to-right return sweep				
Ask the child to circle a word on the page. (Use page with one line of text.)	discriminates between letter and word				
What did the author do to help us find each word? (Use page with one line of text.)	recognizes that words are separated by spaces				
Show me the page where this story ends.	understands text layout				
Date					
Score		___ /10	___ /10	___ /10	___ /10

Record your notes on the back of this page.

Auditory Discrimination Assessment

Environmental Sounds

(Timesaver: Prior to the evaluation, use the props to record commonly heard sounds on audiotape. Then use a tape recorder to play the sound segments for each child, pressing the pause button between the playing sounds and providing wait-time for the child to respond.)

DIRECTIONS

1. Keep the props in the storage box, out of the child's line of sight. (You may find it helpful to place an open, upright file folder between the box and the child to obscure the child's view.)

2. Show the picture cards to the child and ask him or her to examine them.

3. Explain that the child will hear familiar sounds and that the child should listen to each sound carefully and then touch the picture card that corresponds to the sound or sounds.

4. Select one prop and use it to make a familiar sound. You might use the props to create sounds by: leafing through the book's pages, sharpening the pencil in the sharpener, shaking the piggybank, opening and closing the scissors, and winding the kitchen timer to make it tic-tock and ring.

5. Ask the child to touch the picture that matches the sound(s) he or she heard. If the child's behavior demonstrates understanding, circle "yes" in the assessment grid below. If the child makes errors, circle "no."

6. Continue the process until all five props have been sounded.

ASSESSMENT OBJECTIVES

The child can:

❑ Identify environmental sounds

MATERIALS

- a set of picture cards (made from the Teacher Form on page 38) and a copy of this page for use with each child
- a collection of five props that can be kept in a storage box and used to make environmental sounds, including: a hardcover book, a pencil along with a pencil sharpener, a small piggybank with coins inside (a can with coins inside makes a good substitute), scissors, and a wind-up clock (a kitchen timer makes a good substitute)

TEACHER FORM

Prop (Corresponding Sound)	1st Assessment	2nd Assessment	3rd Assessment	4th Assessment
Book (paper pages turning)	YES NO	YES NO	YES NO	YES NO
Pencil Sharpener (a pencil being sharpened)	YES NO	YES NO	YES NO	YES NO
Piggybank and Coins (coins jingling)	YES NO	YES NO	YES NO	YES NO
Scissors (scissors cutting)	YES NO	YES NO	YES NO	YES NO
Wind-Up Timer (a clock tic-tocking)	YES NO	YES NO	YES NO	YES NO
	Date _____	Date _____	Date _____	Date _____

Notes

CHILD'S NAME

AUDITORY DISCRIMINATION ASSESSMENT: ENVIRONMENTAL SOUNDS   TEACHER FORM

DIRECTIONS

Copy this page and laminate it for durability. Cut out the cards along the dashed lines. Store them in a sturdy envelope or self-sealing bag.

Visual Discrimination Assessment

Matching Pictures

ASSESSMENT OBJECTIVES

The child can:
❏ Discriminate between pictures that are the same or different

MATERIALS
- pencils, two blank sheets of paper (for masking), and a copy of this page for use with each child
- a copy of the Student Form (page 40) for each child

DIRECTIONS

1. Explain to the child that he or she will be examining pictures to see which words are the same.

2. Point to the first picture in the sample row and ask the child to mark all the pictures that match it.

3. If the child is successful, repeat the process of having the child examine one line at time and marking the matching picture(s) in the row. If the child makes two successive errors, stop testing.

4. When the Student Form is complete, dismiss the child and examine his or her work. Total the number of rows the child has completed correctly. Record the date and tally below.

TEACHER FORM

1st Assessment	2nd Assessment	3rd Assessment	4th Assessment
Date _____	Date _____	Date _____	Date _____
Score ____ /5	Score ____ /5	Score ____ /5	Score ____ /5

Answer Key　　Sample

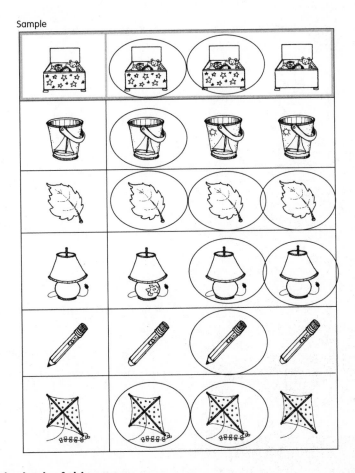

CHILD'S NAME

Record your notes on the back of this page.

VISUAL DISCRIMINATION ASSESSMENT: MATCHING PICTURES

Sample

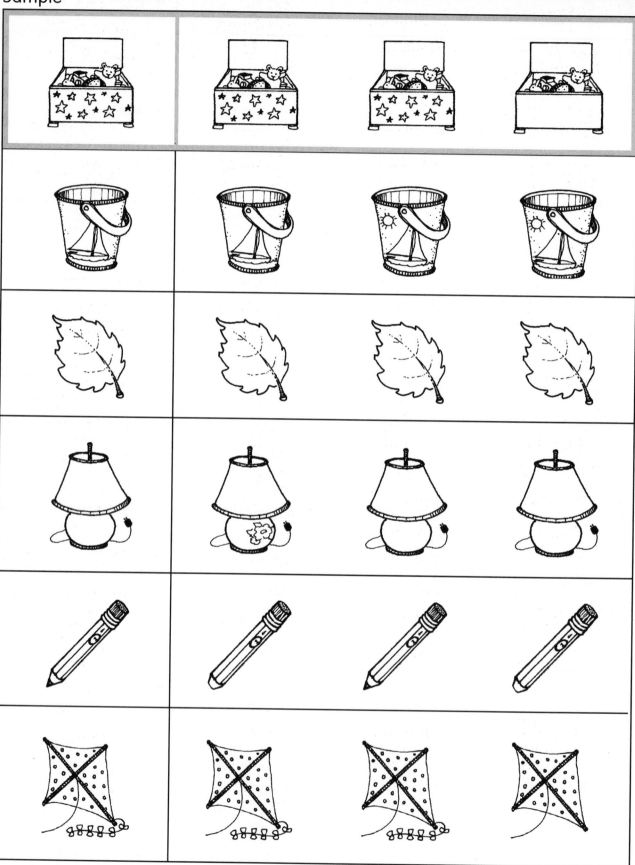

Easy Assessments for Pre-Kindergarten © 2007 Laurie B. Fyke, Scholastic Teaching Resources

Visual Discrimination Assessment

Word Sorting

ASSESSMENT OBJECTIVES

The child can:

❏ Sort words by visual cues (with regard to lengths and initial letters)

MATERIALS

• a set of word cards (made from the Teacher Form on page 42) and a copy of this page for use with each child

DIRECTIONS

Note: These two sorting tasks may be administered separately and at different times.

1. Display the word cards. Ask the child to examine them. Explain that he or she should sort the word cards according to your directions.

2. If the child's sorting behavior demonstrates understanding, circle "yes" in the grid below. (See answer key.) If child makes sorting errors, record your observations on the back of the page.

3. Tell the child to sort the word cards by . . .

   • *length*, grouping long words and short words. You might say "Put all the long words in one group. Then place all the short words in another group."

   • *initial letters*. You might say "Put all the words that start with the same letter in one group. Are there other words that begin with the same letter? If so, put them in them other groups."

TEACHER FORM

Visual Cues	1st Assessment	2nd Assessment	3rd Assessment	4th Assessment
lengths	YES NO	YES NO	YES NO	YES NO
initial letters	YES NO	YES NO	YES NO	YES NO
	Date _____	Date _____	Date _____	Date _____

Answer Key

Visual Cues	Word Cards
lengths	(Grouped in order from shortest to longest) me; ham and hen; kind, love, and tree; doghouse, lunchbox, and railroad; excellent and hamburger; playground and microscope; hippopotamus
initial letters	(Grouped by common initial letter) ham, hamburger, hen, hippopotamus; love, lunchbox; me, microscope

Notes

CHILD'S NAME

DIRECTIONS

Copy this page and laminate it for durability. Cut out the cards along the dashed lines. Store them in a sturdy envelope or self-sealing bag.

kind	hippopotamus
playground	tree
love	excellent
hamburger	lunchbox
doghouse	railroad
me	microscope
ham	hen

Visual Discrimination Assessment

Matching Words

ASSESSMENT OBJECTIVES

The child can:

☐ Discriminate between words that are the same or different

MATERIALS

• pencils, two blank sheets of paper (for masking), and a copy of this page for use with each child

• a copy of the Student Form (page 44) for each child

DIRECTIONS

1. Explain to the child that he or she will be examining words to see which words are the same.

2. Point to the first word in the sample row and ask the child to circle all the words that match that word.

3. If the child is successful, repeat the process of having the child examine one line at time and circling the matching words in the row. If the child makes two successive errors, stop testing.

4. When the Student Form is complete, dismiss the child and examine his or her work. Total the number of rows the child has completed correctly. Record the date and tally below.

TEACHER FORM

1st Assessment	2nd Assessment	3rd Assessment	4th Assessment
Date _____	Date _____	Date _____	Date _____
Score ____ /5	Score ____ /5	Score ____ /5	Score ____ /5

Answer Key

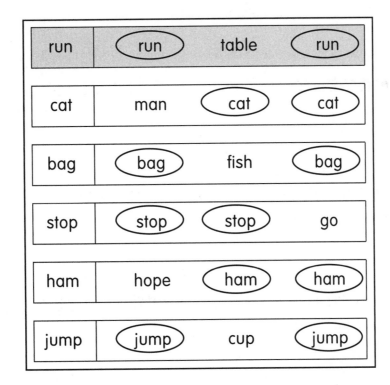

CHILD'S NAME

Record your notes on the back of this page.

Sample	run	run	table	run

	cat	man	cat	cat

	bag	bag	fish	bag

	stop	stop	stop	go

	ham	hope	ham	ham

	jump	jump	cup	jump

   Easy Assessments for Pre-Kindergarten © 2007 Laurie B. Fyke, Scholastic Teaching Resources

Visual Discrimination Assessment

Name Recognition

DIRECTIONS

1. Before giving the Student Form to the child:
   - Write two first names in any of the three-box set. (These names should be somewhat unfamiliar to your students. In other words, they should be names other than those of your students.)
   - Write four first names in any of the five-box set. (These names should be drawn from the first names of other children in the classroom.)
   - Write the first name of the child being assessed in the remaining boxes.

2. Explain to the child that he or she will need to point out his or her name from among other children's names on the Student Form.

3. Tell the child to identify his or her name from the three-box set.

4. If the child's behavior demonstrates understanding, circle "yes" in the grid below and ask the child to identify his or her name from the five-box set. If the child was unsuccessful with the first task, circle "no" in the grid below and stop the assessment.

ASSESSMENT OBJECTIVES

The child can:
- ❏ Identify his or her first name out of three unfamiliar names
- ❏ Identify his or her first name out of five classmates' names

MATERIALS
- a copy of this page for use with each child
- a copy of the Student Form (page 46) for each child

TEACHER FORM

Behaviors or understandings to look for:	1st Assessment	2nd Assessment	3rd Assessment	4th Assessment
Identifies first name among three unfamiliar names.	YES NO	YES NO	YES NO	YES NO
Identifies first name among five classmates' names.	YES NO	YES NO	YES NO	YES NO
	Date _____	Date _____	Date _____	Date _____

CHILD'S NAME

Notes

I can identify my first name.

Visual Discrimination Assessment

Like Letters

DIRECTIONS

1. Explain to the child that he or she will be examining letters to see which are the same or different.
2. Point to the first letter in the sample row and ask the child to circle the letters that are the same.
3. If the child is successful, repeat the process of having the child examine one line at time and circling the matching letters in the row. If the child makes two successive errors, stop testing.
4. Total the number of like letters circled correctly. (See Answer Key.)

Child's Response 1st Assessment	Child's Response 2nd Assessment	Child's Response 3rd Assessment	Child's Response 4th Assessment
Date _____ Score ____ /5	Date _____ Score ____ /5	Date _____ Score ____ /5	Date _____ Score ____ /5

Answer Key

w	v	x	m	(w)	(w)
k	(k)	s	i	(k)	j
p	(p)	(p)	d	g	r
e	c	o	(e)	b	(e)
f	q	(f)	l	(f)	t
h	(h)	n	u	(h)	y

Record your notes on the back of this page.

Sample	w	v	x	m	w	w
	k	k	s	i	k	j
	p	p	p	d	g	r
	e	c	o	e	b	e
	f	q	f	l	f	t
	h	h	n	u	h	y

Phonological Awareness Assessment

Syllables

ASSESSMENT OBJECTIVES

The child can:

❑ Clap and count the number of syllables in a given word

MATERIALS

• a copy of this page for use with each child

DIRECTIONS

1. Explain that you will read a word aloud and that the child should listen carefully.

2. Explain that the child should clap and count the number of syllables (beats) in the word.

3. Provide at least two examples, preferably using the child's name in one example:
   • You might say, "Listen: *pancake*. Clap and count the beats in the word *pan-cake*."
   • If the child's name is Dave you might say, "Listen: *Dave*. Clap and count the beats in the word *Dave*."

4. Begin saying the words and asking the child to clap and count the beats, one word at a time. Note that each word may be said aloud a second time only.

5. Write a checkmark if the child claps and counts the correct number of beats. (See Answer Key.) If the child claps and counts incorrectly, record the child's response below.

TEACHER FORM

Word	Child's Response				Answer Key (syllables)
	1st Assessment	**2nd Assessment**	**3rd Assessment**	**4th Assessment**	
Sample: donut	donut . . . one	do-nu-tuh . . . three	do-nut . . . three	do-nut . . . two	**2**
bear					1
pop-corn					2
ham-bur-ger					3
wa-gon					2
house					1
flash-light					2
el-e-phant					3
dog					1
su-per-mar-ket					4
roo-ster					2
	Date _____ Score ___ /10	Date _____ Score ___ /10	Date _____ Score ___ /10	Date _____ Score ___ /10	

Notes

CHILD'S NAME

Phonological Awareness Assessment

Segmentation of Sentences

ASSESSMENT OBJECTIVES

The child can:

❏ Segment sentences into words

MATERIALS

- 10 one-inch counters and a small container
- a copy of this page for use with each child

DIRECTIONS

1. Distribute the counters and the container to the child.
2. Tell the child that you will read a sentence aloud. Explain that while the child repeats the sentence aloud, he or she should place one counter into the container for each word in the sentence.
   - You might say, "Listen: *I can jump.* Repeat the sentence and count out each word by putting a counter into the container." Then model the action of placing the counters into the container.
   - Repeat this process with the second sample sentence.
3. Read the first sentence prompt, "I like cats."
4. For each counter the child uses correctly, write a checkmark above the corresponding word in the child's response column. If the child makes errors, record them as well. Answers appear in parentheses.

TEACHER FORM

1st Assessment Child's Response	2nd Assessment Child's Response	3rd Assessment Child's Response	4th Assessment Child's Response
(3) I like cats.	I like cats.	I like cats.	I like cats.
(3) We play games.	We play games.	We play games.	We play games.
(2) Look out!	Look out!	Look out!	Look out!
(3) He drinks milk.	He drinks milk.	He drinks milk.	He drinks milk.
(4) She can run fast!	She can run fast!	She can run fast!	She can run fast!
Date _____ Score ____ /5	Date _____ Score ____ /5	Date _____ Score ____ /5	Date _____ Score ____ /5

Notes

Phonological Awareness Assessment

Perceiving Rhyme

ASSESSMENT OBJECTIVES

The child can:

❑ Identify a rhyme

MATERIALS
• a copy of this page for use with each child

DIRECTIONS

1. Explain to the child that he or she should listen carefully while you read pairs of words aloud. Inform the child that you will pause for a moment between the words in each pair.

2. Explain that if the two words have endings that sound similar or rhyme, the child should say "yes." If the words have endings that sound different, the child should say "no." Provide at least two examples:
   • You might say, "Listen: *milk* [pause] *pail*. Do those words have endings that sound similar? Yes or no?"
   • You might say, "Listen: *tease* [pause] *sneeze*. Do those words have endings that sound similar? Yes or no?"

3. Begin saying the word pairs. Note that each pair may be said aloud a second time only.

4. Record the child's response by circling YES or NO in the form below.

TEACHER FORM

Word Pairs		Child's Response 1st Assessment	Child's Response 2nd Assessment	Child's Response 3rd Assessment	Child's Response 4th Assessment	Answer Key
car	star	YES NO	YES NO	YES NO	YES NO	yes
goat	boat	YES NO	YES NO	YES NO	YES NO	yes
farm	cow	YES NO	YES NO	YES NO	YES NO	no
house	mouse	YES NO	YES NO	YES NO	YES NO	yes
rain	train	YES NO	YES NO	YES NO	YES NO	yes
table	toothbrush	YES NO	YES NO	YES NO	YES NO	no
snake	rake	YES NO	YES NO	YES NO	YES NO	yes
bird	tree	YES NO	YES NO	YES NO	YES NO	no
dog	pond	YES NO	YES NO	YES NO	YES NO	no
bear	chair	YES NO	YES NO	YES NO	YES NO	yes
		Date _____	Date _____	Date _____	Date _____	
		Score ____ /10	Score ____ /10	Score ____ /10	Score ____ /10	

CHILD'S NAME

Phonological Awareness Assessment

Making a Rhyme

DIRECTIONS

1. Tell the child that you will say a word aloud and that he or she should listen carefully to its ending.

2. Explain that you will pause for a moment after you say each word so the child can think of a word that rhymes with it. Provide at least two examples:
   • You might say, "Listen: *boat* [pause] Tell me a word that has a similar ending."
   • You might say, "Listen: *snail* [pause] Tell me a word that has a similar ending."

3. Say each of the ten words on the word list, pausing between each word to record the child's response on the Teacher Form. Note that each word may be said aloud a second time only.

TEACHER FORM

Word List	Child's Response 1st Assessment	Child's Response 2nd Assessment	Child's Response 3rd Assessment	Child's Response 4th Assessment
cat				
king				
red				
mad				
pet				
like				
got				
clock				
book				
sun				
	Date _____ Score ____ /10	Date _____ Score ____ /10	Date _____ Score ____ /10	Date _____ Score ____ /10

Notes

 Easy Assessments for Pre-Kindergarten © 2007 Laurie B. Fyke, Scholastic Teaching Resources

Phonological Awareness Assessment

Blending Onsets and Rimes

ASSESSMENT OBJECTIVES

The child can:

❐ Blend onsets and rimes

MATERIALS

• a copy of this page for use with each child

DIRECTIONS

1. Explain that you will say two parts of a word aloud. The child should listen carefully and repeat those sounds in order to say the word. Provide at least two examples:
   • You might say, "What's my word? Listen: *h-ot*."
   • You might say, "What's my word? Listen: *sn-ake*."

2. Say the first onset-rime combination listed on the Teacher Form (*b-ed*). You may say the onset and rime aloud a second time, but a second time only.

3. If the child's response demonstrates understanding, write a checkmark in the grid below. If the child makes errors, record his or her response.

4. Repeat the process until the child has attempted to say all ten words.

TEACHER FORM

Onset-Rime Combination	Child's Response 1st Assessment	Child's Response 2nd Assessment	Child's Response 3rd Assessment	Child's Response 4th Assessment
d-og				
r-ake				
j-ump				
s-and				
b-ang				
f-un				
m-ud				
t-en				
ch-ip				
sh-ape				
	Date _____ Score ____ /10	Date _____ Score ____ /10	Date _____ Score ____ /10	Date _____ Score ____ /10

Notes

CHILD'S NAME

Phonological Awareness Assessment

Letter Names

ASSESSMENT OBJECTIVES

The child can:
❑ Identify the letters in his or her name and other letters

MATERIALS
• two blank sheets of paper (for masking), a copy of this page for use with each child, and a laminated copy of the Student Form (page 55)

DIRECTIONS

1. Explain to the child that he or she will be looking at the letters of the alphabet, many of which may be familiar.
2. Point to a letter on the Student Form that is part of his or her first name.
3. Ask the child to say the letter's name. Note how long it takes the child to answer. If the child finds the task too difficult, stop testing.
4. Write a checkmark on the Teacher Form if the child identifies each of the letters in his or her name correctly. If the child makes an error, record the child's response.
5. Continue the process of pointing to letters and asking the child to name them until he or she has attempted to identify all lower- and uppercase letters or finds the task too difficult.
6. Record the speed with which the child responded overall (slow and/or labored, moderate, fast and/or fluent).

TEACHER FORM

Lowercase Letters

s	m	a	n	i	t	p
e	c	k	r	d	h	o
g	u	f	l	b	j	w
z	v	y	x	q		

Uppercase Letters

A	N	I	T	S	M	C
K	R	D	P	E	G	U
F	L	H	O	Z	Q	X
Y	B	J	W	V		

1st Assessment   Date _____

Lowercase Letter Names   Score ____ /26
Speed: ❑ slow/labored ❑ moderate ❑ fast/fluent

Uppercase Letter Names   Score ____ /26
Speed: ❑ slow/labored ❑ moderate ❑ fast/fluent

Lowercase Letters

s	m	a	n	i	t	p
e	c	k	r	d	h	o
g	u	f	l	b	j	w
z	v	y	x	q		

Uppercase Letters

A	N	I	T	S	M	C
K	R	D	P	E	G	U
F	L	H	O	Z	Q	X
Y	B	J	W	V		

2nd Assessment   Date _____

Lowercase Letter Names   Score ____ /26
Speed: ❑ slow/labored ❑ moderate ❑ fast/fluent

Uppercase Letter Names   Score ____ /26
Speed: ❑ slow/labored ❑ moderate ❑ fast/fluent

Lowercase Letters

s	m	a	n	i	t	p
e	c	k	r	d	h	o
g	u	f	l	b	j	w
z	v	y	x	q		

Uppercase Letters

A	N	I	T	S	M	C
K	R	D	P	E	G	U
F	L	H	O	Z	Q	X
Y	B	J	W	V		

3rd Assessment   Date _____

Lowercase Letter Names   Score ____ /26
Speed: ❑ slow/labored ❑ moderate ❑ fast/fluent

Uppercase Letter Names   Score ____ /26
Speed: ❑ slow/labored ❑ moderate ❑ fast/fluent

Lowercase Letters

s	m	a	n	i	t	p
e	c	k	r	d	h	o
g	u	f	l	b	j	w
z	v	y	x	q		

Uppercase Letters

A	N	I	T	S	M	C
K	R	D	P	E	G	U
F	L	H	O	Z	Q	X
Y	B	J	W	V		

4th Assessment   Date _____

Lowercase Letter Names   Score ____ /26
Speed: ❑ slow/labored ❑ moderate ❑ fast/fluent

Uppercase Letter Names   Score ____ /26
Speed: ❑ slow/labored ❑ moderate ❑ fast/fluent

Record your notes on the back of this page.

PHONOLOGICAL AWARENESS ASSESSMENT: LETTER NAMES

DIRECTIONS

Copy this page and laminate it for durability.

s	m	a	n	i	t	p
e	c	k	r	d	h	o
g	u	f	l	b	j	w
z	v	y	x	q		

A	N	I	T	S	M	C
K	R	D	P	E	G	U
F	L	H	O	X	Q	X
Y	B	J	W	V		

Phonemic Awareness Assessment

Letter Sounds

ASSESSMENT OBJECTIVES

The child can:

❏ Recognize and say the sound of letters in his or her name and other letters

MATERIALS

• two blank sheets of paper (for masking), a copy of this page and page 54 for use with each child, and a laminated copy of the Student Form (page 58)

DIRECTIONS

1. Explain to the child that he or she will be identifying letter sounds.
2. Point to a letter on the Student Form that is part of his or her first name.
3. Ask the child to look at the letter and say the sound(s) associated with that letter. Note how long it takes the child to answer. If the child finds the task too difficult, stop testing. (Allow children who say a long-vowel sound to try saying the short-vowel sound. You might say, "Sometimes letters that are vowels say their own names, but what other sound do you think of when you see this letter?")
4. Write a checkmark on the Teacher Form if the child identifies the consonant and vowel sounds in his or her name correctly. If the child makes an error, record the child's response.
5. Continue the process of pointing to letters and asking the child to say the sounds associated with them until he or she has attempted to identify all consonant and short-vowel sounds.
6. Record the speed with which the child responded overall (slow and/or labored, moderate, fast and/or fluent).

TEACHER FORM

Sample Assessment

Letter Sounds (Lowercase)

s ✓	m ✓	a	n ✓	i	t ✓
sit	man	pan	net	sip	tent
p ✓	e	c ✓	k ✓	r	d
pin	leg	cat	kite	red	dog
h	o	g ✓	u ✓	f ✓	l ✓
hop	lot	go	cup	fan	lite
b	j ✓	w	z ✓	v ✓	y
bed	job	web	zoo	van	yak
x ✓			qu		
box /ks/			queen /kw/		

1st Assessment   Date ___9/19___

Lowercase ✓ Score __15__ /26

Speed: ☑ slow/labored ❏ moderate ❏ fast/fluent

Letter Sounds (Lowercase)

s	m	a	n	i	t
sit	man	pan	net	sip	tent
p	e	c	k	r	d
pin	leg	cat	kite	red	dog
h	o	g	u	f	l
hop	lot	go	cup	fan	lite
b	j	w	z	v	y
bed	job	web	zoo	van	yak
x			qu		
box /ks/			queen /kw/		

Letter Sounds (Uppercase)

A	N	I	T	S	M
pan	net	sip	tent	sit	man
C	R	D	K	P	E
cat	red	dog	kite	pin	leg
G	U	F	L	H	O
go	cup	fan	lite	hop	lot
W	Z	V	Y	B	J
web	zoo	van	yak	bed	job
QU			X		
queen /kw/			box /ks/		

1st Assessment   Date _____

Lowercase   Score ____ /26

Speed: ❏ slow/labored ❏ moderate ❏ fast/fluent

Uppercase   Score ____ /26

Speed: ❏ slow/labored ❏ moderate ❏ fast/fluent

Letter Sounds (Lowercase)

s sit	m man	a pan	n net	i sip	t tent
p pin	e leg	c cat	k kite	r red	d dog
h hop	o lot	g go	u cup	f fan	l lite
b bed	j job	w web	z zoo	v van	y yak
x box /ks/			qu queen /kw/		

Letter Sounds (Uppercase)

A pan	N net	I sip	T tent	S sit	M man
C cat	R red	D dog	K kite	P pin	E leg
G go	U cup	F fan	L lite	H hop	O lot
W web	Z zoo	V van	Y yak	B bed	J job
QU queen /kw/			X box /ks/		

2nd Assessment   Date _____

Lowercase   Score ____ /26   Uppercase   Score ____ /26

Speed: ❑ slow/labored ❑ moderate ❑ fast/fluent   Speed: ❑ slow/labored ❑ moderate ❑ fast/fluent

---

Letter Sounds (Lowercase)

s sit	m man	a pan	n net	i sip	t tent
p pin	e leg	c cat	k kite	r red	d dog
h hop	o lot	g go	u cup	f fan	l lite
b bed	j job	w web	z zoo	v van	y yak
x box /ks/			qu queen /kw/		

Letter Sounds (Uppercase)

A pan	N net	I sip	T tent	S sit	M man
C cat	R red	D dog	K kite	P pin	E leg
G go	U cup	F fan	L lite	H hop	O lot
W web	Z zoo	V van	Y yak	B bed	J job
QU queen /kw/			X box /ks/		

3rd Assessment   Date _____

Lowercase   Score ____ /26   Uppercase   Score ____ /26

Speed: ❑ slow/labored ❑ moderate ❑ fast/fluent   Speed: ❑ slow/labored ❑ moderate ❑ fast/fluent

---

Letter Sounds (Lowercase)

s sit	m man	a pan	n net	i sip	t tent
p pin	e leg	c cat	k kite	r red	d dog
h hop	o lot	g go	u cup	f fan	l lite
b bed	j job	w web	z zoo	v van	y yak
x box /ks/			qu queen /kw/		

Letter Sounds (Uppercase)

A pan	N net	I sip	T tent	S sit	M man
C cat	R red	D dog	K kite	P pin	E leg
G go	U cup	F fan	L lite	H hop	O lot
W web	Z zoo	V van	Y yak	B bed	J job
QU queen /kw/			X box /ks/		

4th Assessment   Date _____

Lowercase   Score ____ /26   Uppercase   Score ____ /26

Speed: ❑ slow/labored ❑ moderate ❑ fast/fluent   Speed: ❑ slow/labored ❑ moderate ❑ fast/fluent

PHONEMIC AWARENESS ASSESSMENT: LETTER SOUNDS

DIRECTIONS

Copy this page and laminate it for durability.

s	m	a	n	i	t
p	e	c	k	r	d
h	o	g	u	f	l
b	j	w	z	v	y
x	qu				

A	N	I	T	S	M
C	R	D	K	P	E
G	U	F	L	H	O
W	Z	V	Y	B	J
Qu	X				

Easy Assessments for Pre-Kindergarten © 2007 Laurie B. Fyke, Scholastic Teaching Resources

Phonemic Awareness Assessment

Isolation of Sounds

DIRECTIONS

1. Tell the child that you will read a word aloud and that he or she should listen carefully.

2. Explain that you will ask the child to tell you what sound is at the beginning or end of each word. Provide at least two examples:
   - You might say, "Listen: *cake* [pause]. What sound do you hear at the beginning of this word?"
   - You might say, "Listen: *map* [pause]. What sound do you hear at the end of this word?"

3. Say each word aloud. Note that each word may be said aloud a second time only.

4. If the child identifies the correct sound, write a checkmark on the Teacher Form.

ASSESSMENT OBJECTIVES

The child can:
❏ Identify the beginning and ending sound of words

MATERIALS
- a copy of this page for use with each child

TEACHER FORM

Word Groups	Child's Response 1st Assessment	Child's Response 2nd Assessment	Child's Response 3rd Assessment	Child's Response 4th Assessment	Answer Key (Common Sound)
BEGINNING SOUNDS					
cat					/c/
game					/g/
wagon					/w/
big					/b/
house					/h/
ENDING SOUNDS					
cup					/p/
dress					/s/
goat					/t/
swim					/m/
seal					/l/
	Date _____ Score ____ /10	Date _____ Score ____ /10	Date _____ Score ____ /10	Date _____ Score ____ /10	

CHILD'S NAME

Notes

Phonemic Awareness Assessment

Matching Sounds

ASSESSMENT OBJECTIVES

The child can:

❑ Match words that begin or end with the same sound

MATERIALS

• a set of picture cards (made from the Teacher Form on page 61) and a copy of this page for use with each child

DIRECTIONS

1. Explain to the child that you will show two picture cards. The child should look at the pictures and then tell you if the two picture cards (or words) begin with the same sound.

2. Display the first pair of cards (see chart below for guidance).

3. Tell the child to examine the pictures. You might say, "Listen carefully. Do these two words start with the same sound: *hat, house* [pause] *hat, house?*"

4. Circle the child's response on the Teacher Form. Repeat step 3 for each pair of words.

5. Repeat the process as above, but this time have the child determine whether the picture pairs can be identified as words that end with the same sound.

TEACHER FORM

Groupings		Child's Response 1st Assessment		Child's Response 2nd Assessment		Child's Response 3rd Assessment		Child's Response 4th Assessment	
Beginning Sounds									
ball, boat	(Yes)	YES	NO	YES	NO	YES	NO	YES	NO
hat, bag	(No)	YES	NO	YES	NO	YES	NO	YES	NO
hook, house	(Yes)	YES	NO	YES	NO	YES	NO	YES	NO
fish, turtle	(No)	YES	NO	YES	NO	YES	NO	YES	NO
pencil, pig	(Yes)	YES	NO	YES	NO	YES	NO	YES	NO
Ending Sounds									
hat, boat	(Yes)	YES	NO	YES	NO	YES	NO	YES	NO
bag, pig	(Yes)	YES	NO	YES	NO	YES	NO	YES	NO
turtle, hook	(No)	YES	NO	YES	NO	YES	NO	YES	NO
pencil, ball	(Yes)	YES	NO	YES	NO	YES	NO	YES	NO
hat, house	(No)	YES	NO	YES	NO	YES	NO	YES	NO
		Date _____		Date _____		Date _____		Date _____	
		Score ____ /10		Score ____ /10		Score ____ /10		Score ____ /10	

Record your notes on the back of this page.

PHONEMIC AWARENESS ASSESSMENT: MATCHING SOUNDS

DIRECTIONS

Copy this page and laminate it for durability. Cut out the cards along the dashed lines. Store them in a sturdy envelope or self-sealing bag.

Phonemic Awareness Assessment

Blending Phonemes

ASSESSMENT OBJECTIVES

The child can:

❐ Blend phonemes together
 to say VC, CV, CVC,
 and CCVC words

V = vowel   C = consonant

MATERIALS

• a copy of this page for use with
 each child

DIRECTIONS

1. Explain that you will be saying the sounds in words, one by one. The child should blend or string together the sounds to say the word as a whole. You might say: "I will slowly stretch out a word. Your job is to repeat each sound in the same order and then push the sounds together to say the word as a whole. Listen as I practice with a few words." Then, use the following examples:
/s/ /a/ /m/ . . . Sam (Preferably, use the child's own name.)
/a/ /t/ . . . at
/p/ /i/ /n/ . . . pin

2. Read the first word on the word list, saying each sound in the word slowly, separately, and clearly. Note: Be sure to say the sounds, not the letters, in the word. If the child experiences difficulty completing the task, try saying the first sound loudly and follow with the other sounds as before.

3. Write a checkmark on the Teacher Form if the child says the word correctly. If child makes an error, record the error and your observations on the back of the page.

4. Repeat the process until the child has attempted to say (blend) all the words.

TEACHER FORM

Word List	Blend	Child's Responses				Answer Key
		1st Assessment	2nd Assessment	3rd Assessment	4th Assessment	
/s/ /a/ /d/	CVC					sad
/b/ /u/ /g/	CVC					bug
/i/ /t/	VC					it
/p/ /e/ /n/	CVC					pen
/s/ /t/ /o/ /p/	CCVC					stop
		Date _____	Date _____	Date _____	Date _____	
		Score ___ /5	Score ___ /5	Score ___ /5	Score ___ /5	

Notes

Phonemic Awareness Assessment

Segmentation of Words

ASSESSMENT OBJECTIVES

The child can:

❏ Segment simple words into phonemes

MATERIALS

• 10 one-inch counters and a copy of this page for use with each child

DIRECTIONS

1. Explain that you will read a word aloud. The child should say the same word and then repeat it again slowly, stretching the word out sound by sound. While he or she says the word, the child should move a block to represent each sound.

2. Distribute the counters and provide at least three examples:

   • You might prompt, "Say: *see*. Now say it again, stretching the word out sound by sound." (A child may respond by saying the /s/ sound and then the /long e/ sound and moving a block for each.)

   • You might prompt, "Say: *cat*. Now say it again, stretching the word out sound by sound." (A child may respond by saying the /k/ sound, the short /a/ sound, and then the /t/ sound, moving a block for each.)

   • You might prompt, "Say: *pit*. Now say it again, stretching the word out sound by sound." (A child may respond by saying the /p/ sound, the short /i/ sound, and then the /t/ sound, moving a block for each.)

3. On the Teacher Form, record a checkmark above each correctly spoken, isolated sound.

TEACHER FORM

Words	Child's Response 1st Assessment	Child's Response 2nd Assessment	Child's Response 3rd Assessment	Child's Response 4th Assessment	Answer Key (segmented sounds)
dog	d o g	d o g	d o g	d o g	/d/ /o/ /g/
can	c a n	c a n	c a n	c a n	/c/ /a/ /n/
up	u p	u p	u p	u p	/u/ /p/
feet	f ee t	f ee t	f ee t	f ee t	/f/ /long e/ /t/
ship	sh i p	sh i p	sh i p	sh i p	/sh/ /i/ /p/
	Date _____ Score ____ /5	Date _____ Score ____ /5	Date _____ Score ____ /5	Date _____ Score ____ /5	

Notes

Reading Assessment:

Read Original Writing

DIRECTIONS

1. Explain to the child that he or she will be drawing a picture and writing about it.

2. Provide the child with a pencil and the Student Form.

3. Ask the child to draw a picture to tell a story. If the child is ready, encourage him or her to write a story about the picture. (Allow the child to move back and forth between the drawing and writing process.)

4. When the child indicates that he or she has completed the task, ask the child to share the story with you. (For future reference, record the child's story in the Notes section or the back of this page.)

5. When the assessment is complete, use the grid below to record the skill(s) the child has demonstrated. (See the *Continuum of Writing Stages* on page 23 for guidance on evaluation.)

ASSESSMENT OBJECTIVES

The child can:

❏ Use emergent reading skills to read his or her original writing

❏ Read simple CVC words from their writing

❏ Demonstrate that writing includes pictures, letters, and words to communicate information and meaning

MATERIALS

• pencils and a copy of this page for use with each child

• a copy of the Student Form (page 65) for each child

TEACHER FORM

Writing Skills *The child is able to:*	1st Assessment	2nd Assessment	3rd Assessment	4th Assessment
Connect the story and the picture by retelling the story orally				
Create meaning from random scribbles or marks				
Read phonetic spellings				
Read with expression				
	Date _____ Score ____ /5	Date _____ Score ____ /5	Date _____ Score ____ /5	Date _____ Score ____ /5

Notes

I can draw a picture and tell about my story.

CHILD'S NAME

DATE

Reading Assessment

Comprehension

ASSESSMENT OBJECTIVES

The child can:
❏ Use listening skills to comprehend a sentence

MATERIALS

• pencils and a copy of this page for use with each child
• a copy of the Student Form (page 67) for each child

DIRECTIONS

1. Explain to the child that you will read a sentence aloud. When you finish reading, you will ask him or her to answer a question about the sentence. Explain that the child may use the pictures on the Student Form for support.
2. Read the sample sentence listed on the Teacher Form (*He can see a big frog.*)
3. Read the sample question listed on the Teacher Form (*What can he see?*)
4. Ask the child to look at the sample box and then mark the picture that best answers that question.
5. Write a checkmark on the teacher form if he or she demonstrates an understanding of the sentence read aloud. If child makes an error, record the child's response. If he or she finds the task too difficult overall, stop testing.
6. Repeat the process until the child has attempted to respond to all five questions.

TEACHER FORM

Sentence	Question	Child's Responses			
Sample: **He can see a big frog.**	**What can he see?**	1st Assessment	2nd Assessment	3rd Assessment	4th Assessment
They found a black cat.	What did they find?				
She likes to kick the ball.	What will she kick?				
He brought a net with him.	What did he bring with him?				
		Date _____	Date _____	Date _____	Date _____

Answer Key

Notes

CHILD'S NAME

DATE

Organizing Information

DIRECTIONS

Note: You may administer this assessment in a large- or small-group setting.

Part A

1. Before distributing the Student Form, explain that you need students to provide directions on how to draw a person.

2. With student direction, model drawing a self-portrait on the chalkboard or other surface. Discuss the positioning of limbs and details while you draw.

3. As a group, discuss attributes of the finished drawing. After the discussion, erase the drawing.

Part B

4. Provide each child with a pencil and Student Form.

5. Explain that students will each draw a self-portrait.

6. Observe each child's pencil grip and hand preference as he or she draws. (See the *Continuum of Writing Stages* on page 23 for guidance on evaluation.)

7. Invite children who have finished drawing to write a message on their papers.

8. Record on the Teacher Form whether each child's behaviors or understandings meet the objectives of this assessment. Note the development of figure drawing and degree of details (See *Children's Drawings as Indicators* on page 25).

ASSESSMENT OBJECTIVES

The child can:

❏ Draw a self-portrait

❏ Demonstrate organizational skills using arrangement of picture details, text, and position on page

❏ Demonstrate an established hand preference.

❏ Demonstrate a correct pencil grip

MATERIALS

- pencils and a copy of this page for use with each child
- a copy of the Student Form (page 69) for each child

TEACHER FORM

Behaviors or understandings to look for:	1st Assessment	2nd Assessment	3rd Assessment	4th Assessment
The self-portrait demonstrates an age-appropriate development of figure drawing.				
The self-portrait provides evidence of organizational skills.				
The child has an established hand preference. (Record R for right or L for left.)				
The child demonstrates a correct pencil grip.				
	Date _____	Date _____	Date _____	Date _____

Notes

I can draw a picture of me.

CHILD'S NAME

DATE

Writing Assessment

Printing Familiar Letters

DIRECTIONS

Note: You may administer this assessment in a small-group setting.

1. Provide the child with a pencil and the Student Form.

2. Ask the child to print the letters in his or her first name on the first line.

3. If the child seems ready, explain that he or she will have several minutes to print more letters and words, as many as he or she is able. If the child is reluctant, suggest that he or she write names of family members, word wall words, words from classroom charts, or high-frequency words (e.g., *my, go, is*).

4. Encourage the child to write as much as possible. If the child needs more space for writing, invite him or her to use the back of the Student Form. (Note: Rather than informing the child about the time constraint, provide him or her with ten minutes to write. The child may find it helpful if you give a five-minute warning and a one-minute-to-go warning before the time is up.)

5. Record on the Teacher Form whether the child's writing behaviors meet the objectives of this assessment. Notice that one child will make random marks and scribbles while another will fill a page. (See the *Continuum of Writing Stages* on page 23 for guidance on evaluation.) Fill in the Teacher Form with additional behaviors or understandings you wish to look for, including left-to-right direction, pencil grip, hand preference, legibility, letter formation, reversals, letter confusion, spacing, complexity of words, and organization of written work.

ASSESSMENT OBJECTIVES

The child can:

❏ Print his or her first name legibly

❏ Use knowledge of alphabet to write or copy letters or words legibly

❏ Use phonic knowledge to spell simple words

MATERIALS

• pencils, a wristwatch, and a copy of this page for use with each child

• a copy of the Student Form (page 71) for each child

TEACHER FORM

Behaviors or understandings to look for:	1st Assessment	2nd Assessment	3rd Assessment	4th Assessment
legible printing of the letters in first name				
legible printing of letters or words				
uses phonic knowledge to spell simple words				
	Date _____	Date _____	Date _____	Date _____

WRITING ASSESSMENT: PRINTING FAMILIAR LETTERS

I can print my name.

_____

I can print other words, too.

_____

_____

_____

_____

_____

CHILD'S INITIALS _____

DATE _____

Interactive and Shared Writing

ASSESSMENT OBJECTIVES

The child can:

❏ Contribute ideas during an interactive writing activity

MATERIALS

- markers and chart paper
- a copy of the Student Form (page 71) for each small group.

DIRECTIONS

Note: Administer this assessment in small-group setting.

Part A

1. Determine the type of collaborative writing with which you'd like children to participate. (The following activities work well for this kind of assessment: cloze activities, experience charts, graphic organizers, graphs, poems, songs, stories, and "Thank You" notes.)

2. Divide the class into a few groups. While you lead one group through this writing assessment, have the rest of the class take part in other instructional activities.

Part B

3. Record the date, type of activity, and group members' names on the Teacher Form.

4. Invite children to volunteer ideas and share feelings, knowledge, reflections, and so on.

5. Encourage both oral and written participation. Guide each child through the interactive writing process as he or she contributes ideas (and drawings or words) to the chart.

6. Record each child's contribution(s) on the Teacher Form. (See the *Continuum of Writing Stages* on page 23 for guidance on evaluation of writing behaviors.)

Sample Assessment

WRITING ASSESSMENT: INTERACTIVE AND SHARED WRITING — LANGUAGE ARTS — TEACHER FORM

Date_____ Activity _Creating an Invitation_

List group members names below.	Contribution	Assessment Objective *During a shared writing experience, the child can:*
Amanda	It's a party	☑ contribute ideas ❏ other
Notes *A suggested the type of event.*		
Tim	Say its a birthday party	☑ contribute ideas ❏ other
Notes *T offered clarification.*		
		❏ contribute ideas ❏ other
Notes		

WRITING ASSESSMENT: INTERACTIVE AND SHARED WRITING

Date_____ Activity _____

List group members' names below.	Contribution	Assessment Objective *During a shared writing experience, the child can:*
		❑ contribute ideas ❑ other
Notes		
		❑ contribute ideas ❑ other
Notes		
		❑ contribute ideas ❑ other
Notes		
		❑ contribute ideas ❑ other
Notes		
		❑ contribute ideas ❑ other
Notes		
		❑ contribute ideas ❑ other
Notes		
		❑ contribute ideas ❑ other
Notes		
		❑ contribute ideas ❑ other
Notes		
		❑ contribute ideas ❑ other
Notes		
		❑ contribute ideas ❑ other
Notes		

Writing Assessment

Risk Taking

DIRECTIONS

Note: You may administer this assessment in a large- or small-group setting.

1. Explain to the children that they will be drawing a picture.

2. Invite children to share with you any questions they have about completing the task. (Record each child's questions with your observations.)

3. Provide each child with a pencil and a copy of the Student Form.

4. In the box on their form, have children draw a picture that tells a message or shares a story. You might say, "It could be a picture that shows people you know, an adventure you went on, or maybe something you read in a book."

5. Encourage children who are ready to write about the picture. (If children need more space for writing, invite them to use the back of the Student Form.) (See the *Continuum of Writing Stages* on page 23 for guidance on evaluation.)

ASSESSMENT OBJECTIVES

The child can:

❏ Express ideas

❏ Use emergent forms of writing to record ideas

❏ Write using an assortment of tools

MATERIALS

• pencils and a copy of this page for use with each child

• a copy of the Student Form (page 75) for each child

TEACHER FORM

Skill Area	1st Assessment	2nd Assessment	3rd Assessment	4th Assessment
		Circle all that apply.		
Express ideas by . . .	describing dictating drawing pictures storytelling other _____	describing dictating drawing pictures storytelling other _____	describing dictating drawing pictures storytelling other _____	describing dictating drawing pictures storytelling other _____
Use emergent forms of writing to record ideas	conventional spelling letter-like marks phonetic spelling random letters scribble symbols other _____	conventional spelling letter-like marks phonetic spelling random letters scribble symbols other _____	conventional spelling letter-like marks phonetic spelling random letters scribble symbols other _____	conventional spelling letter-like marks phonetic spelling random letters scribble symbols other _____
Write using an assortment of tools	chalk crayons markers pencils stamps other _____	chalk crayons markers pencils stamps other _____	chalk crayons markers pencils stamps other _____	chalk crayons markers pencils stamps other _____
	Date _____	Date _____	Date _____	Date _____

WRITING ASSESSMENT: RISK TAKING

CHILD'S NAME

DATE

Writing Assessment

Communicating Ideas

DIRECTIONS

Part A

1. As a large group, brainstorm about writing. Encourage children to talk about writing for different purposes.
   - You might say, "Why do you think some people like to write things down on paper?" (e.g., *to tell stories, make lists, record information*)
2. Invite children to talk about different formats of writing.
   - You might say, "What kinds or writing have you done or seen people do?" (e.g., *writing in journals, posters,* or *storybooks*)
3. Record and categorize student responses with a chart or graphic organizer.
4. Divide the class into a few groups. While you lead one group through this assessment, have the rest of the class take part in other instructional activities.

Part B

5. Ask children to provide information as you model how to complete a template using pictures or other forms of emergent writing. Talk about ways they can copy words from around the room.
6. Provide children with numerous and varied writing materials and tools. Invite children to use the template at a work station. Reproducible templates for writing letters, award certificates, and recipes have been provided for you (See Student Forms). Use them to complement your own collection of writing tools and templates.
7. Acknowledge and accept all emergent forms of writing for this assessment. (See the *Continuum of Writing Stages* on page 23 for guidance on evaluation.)

ASSESSMENT OBJECTIVES

The child can:

❏ Perform emergent writing in a variety of formats

List all that apply:

_____

_____

_____

❏ Perform emergent writing in a variety of genres

List all that apply:

_____

_____

_____

MATERIALS

- a variety of writing tools and materials (e.g., stationery, blank journals, markers, crayons); and a copy of this page for use with each child
- a copy of one of the Student Forms (pages 77–79) for each child

TEACHER FORM

1st Assessment	2nd Assessment	3rd Assessment	4th Assessment
Date _____	Date _____	Date _____	Date _____

Record your notes on the back of this page.

Dear _____ ,

_____

_____

_____

_____

Sincerely,

_____

CHILD'S NAME

DATE

Congratulations!

To:

This award is being given because . . .

From:

LANGUAGE ARTS

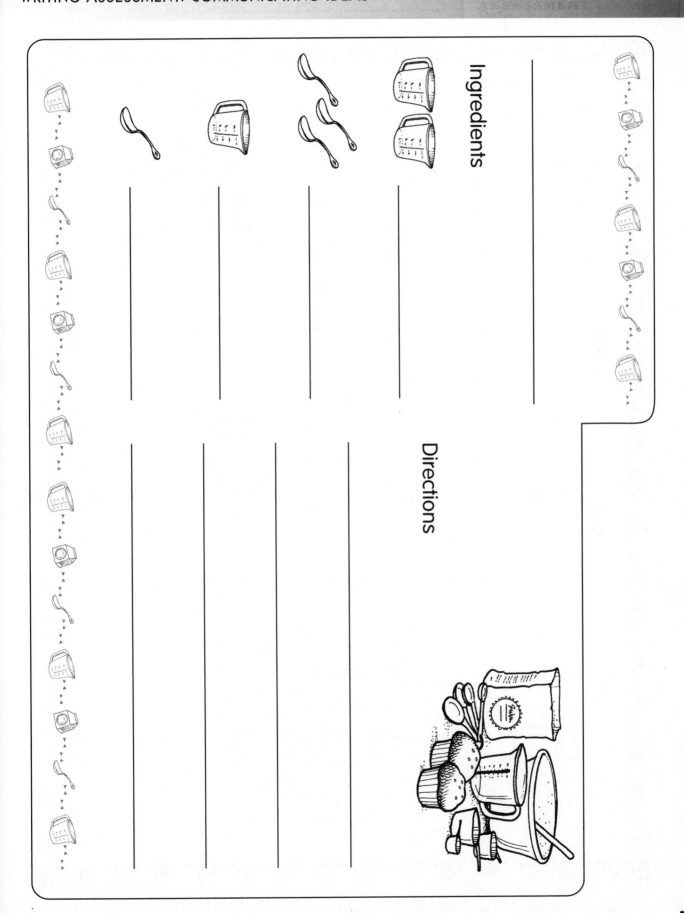

Ingredients

Directions

CHILD'S NAME

DATE

Mathematics

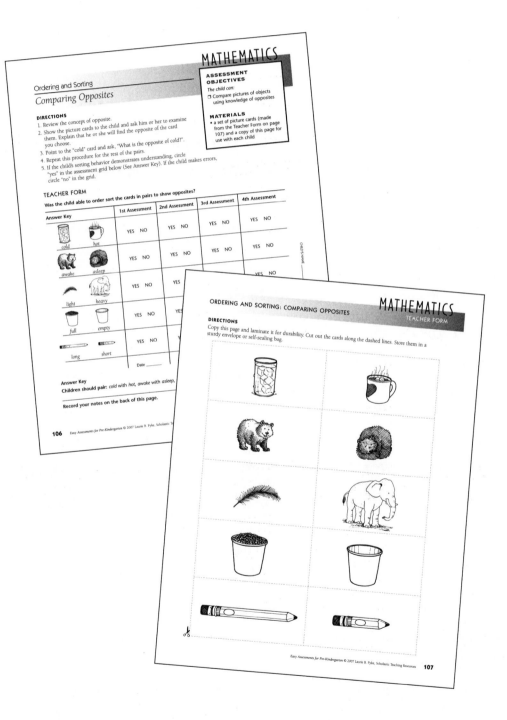

Ordering and Sorting
Comparing Opposites

MATHEMATICS

ASSESSMENT OBJECTIVES

The child can:
☐ Compare pictures of objects using knowledge of opposites

MATERIALS
• a set of picture cards (made from the Teacher Form on page 107) and a copy of this page for use with each child

DIRECTIONS
1. Review the concept of opposite.
2. Show the picture cards to the child and ask him or her to examine them. Explain that he or she will find the opposite of the card you choose.
3. Point to the "cold" card and ask, "What is the opposite of cold?".
4. Repeat this procedure for the rest of the pairs.
5. If the child's sorting behavior demonstrates understanding, circle "yes" in the assessment grid below (See Answer Key). If the child makes errors, circle "no" in the grid.

TEACHER FORM

Was the child able to order sort the cards in pairs to show opposites?

Answer Key	1st Assessment	2nd Assessment	3rd Assessment	4th Assessment
cold / hot	YES NO	YES NO	YES NO	YES NO
awake / asleep	YES NO	YES NO	YES NO	YES NO
light / heavy	YES NO	YES		
full / empty	YES NO	YES		
long / short	YES NO	YES		
			Date _____	

Answer Key
Children should pair: cold with *hot*, awake with *asleep*,

Record your notes on the back of this page.

ORDERING AND SORTING: COMPARING OPPOSITES

MATHEMATICS
TEACHER FORM

DIRECTIONS
Copy this page and laminate it for durability. Cut out the cards along the dashed lines. Store them in a sturdy envelope or self-sealing bag.

Introduction to Mathematics

Use the resources and materials noted below to help you support all learners and evaluate learning in the following areas: shapes; numeration; ordering and sorting; measurement, time, and money; spatial relationships and terminology; operation and place value; and, charts and graphs.

Resources for Helping Kids Who Struggle With Math

Read about how you can better serve students who have difficulty learning math.

Geary, D. C. (2003). Learning disabilities in arithmetic. In H. L. Swanson, K. R. Harris, & S. Graham (Eds.), *Handbook of learning disabilities* (199–212). New York: Guilford.

Gersten, R., Jordan, N., and Flojo, J. R. (2005). Early identification and interventions for students with mathematics difficulties. *Journal of Learning Disabilities*, 38, 293–304.

Hallahan, D. P., Lloyd, J. W. Kauffman, J. M., Weiss, M., and Martinez, E. A. (2005). *Learning disabilities: Foundations, characteristics, and effective teaching.* Boston: Allyn and Bacon.

Best Practice Tips

- Model math concepts that may be unfamiliar to students by using concrete materials (e.g., buttons, play clay, measuring tools). Invite children to manipulate the materials frequently, giving opportunities to strengthen and scaffold learning.

- Think out loud! Give children a window into your thought processes by sharing aloud how you approach new ideas and materials, access prior knowledge, and solve problems.

- Build skills through play. Educational play provides children with authentic reasons to use and extend their math knowledge. It provides opportunities to practice important skills and behaviors related to exploration, experimentation, investigation, and more.

CONNECTIONS TO THE MATH STANDARDS

National Council for Teachers of Mathematics (NCTM) has proposed what teachers should provide for their students to become proficient in mathematics.
To learn how the math assessments in this book support these standards for pre-kindergarten, visit the Web site: http://standards.nctm.org.
For additional information about NCTM and to learn more about the topics and benchmarks within each math standard, read *Principles and Standards for School Mathematics* from the National Council for Teachers of Mathematics, 2000.

Assessment Category	Page	Assessment Tool Title	Number and Operations	Algebra	Geometry	Measurement	Data Analysis and Probability	Problem Solving	Reasoning and Proof	Communication	Connections	Representation
SHAPES	91	Properties and Relationships			✓			✓	✓	✓	✓	✓
NUMERATION	93	Recognizing Numerals	✓									✓
	96	Quantity and Correspondence	✓					✓			✓	✓
	98	Comparing Sets by Number	✓				✓	✓	✓	✓	✓	✓
ORDERING & SORTING	100	Comparing Sets by Attributes	✓		✓	✓		✓	✓	✓		
	102	Smallest to Largest		✓		✓		✓	✓	✓	✓	✓
	104	Three Stages of Development		✓		✓		✓	✓	✓	✓	✓
	106	Comparing Opposites		✓		✓		✓	✓	✓	✓	✓
	108	Simple Patterns		✓		✓		✓	✓	✓	✓	✓
MEASUREMENT, TIME, & MONEY	111	Comparing Length, Weight, and Capacity				✓		✓	✓	✓	✓	✓
	113	Matching Tools and Traits				✓		✓	✓	✓	✓	✓
	115	Using Time Vocabulary	✓			✓		✓	✓	✓	✓	✓
	117	Matching Coins	✓			✓		✓	✓	✓	✓	✓
SPATIAL RELATIONSHIPS & TERMINOLOGY	119	Relative Positions		✓		✓		✓	✓	✓	✓	✓
OPERATION & PLACE VALUE	121	Math Stories	✓			✓		✓	✓	✓	✓	✓
	124	Dictated Math Stories	✓	✓		✓		✓	✓	✓	✓	✓
CHARTS & GRAPHS	126	Collecting and Analyzing Data	✓			✓	✓	✓	✓	✓	✓	✓

MATHEMATICS LEARNING EXPECTATIONS

By the end of the school year, a pre-kindergartner should begin to . . .

	Scope and Sequence Guidelines Time Line (Spanning Ten Months)			
	1	2	3	4
SHAPES				
Recognize and identify simple geometric shapes.	X	X	X	X
Compare and describe two-dimensional geometric shapes using common attributes.		X	X	X
Recognize and identify geometric shapes in the environment.				
NUMERATION				
Recognize and identify the numerals from 0–9.	X	X	X	X
Rote count by ones from 0–10 or higher.	X	X	X	X
Count objects to match numerals (0–10).				X
Establish a one-to-one correspondence by counting objects while saying aloud the number word.	X	X	X	X
Compare and identify sets that contain up to five objects.			X	X
ORDERING AND SORTING				
Sort, classify, and order sets according to the attributes of shape, size, and color.			X	X
Order objects according to size.	X	X	X	X
Sequence three stages of development.	X	X	X	X
Compare pictures of objects using knowledge of opposites.				X
Identify, copy, and repeat simple patterns (e.g., ab, abc, aabb).	X	X	X	X

Scope and Sequence Guidelines						Evaluation and Support	
Time Line (Spanning Ten Months)						Assessment Tool Page	Send-Home Card Page
5	6	7	8	9	10		
X						91	154
X	X	X	X	X	X	91	154
X	X	X	X	X	X	91	154
X	X	X	X	X	X	93	155
X	X	X	X	X	X	93	
X	X	X	X	X	X	96	155, 160
X	X	X	X	X	X	96	155, 160
X	X	X	X	X	X	98	163
X	X	X	X	X	X	100	155, 156
X	X	X				102	155, 156
X	X	X				104	
X	X	X	X	X	X	106	
X	X	X	X	X	X	108	156

MATHEMATICS LEARNING EXPECTATIONS

By the end of the school year, a pre-kindergartner should begin to . . .

	Scope and Sequence Guidelines Time Line (Spanning Ten Months)			
	1	2	3	4
MEASUREMENT, TIME, AND MONEY				
Compare length, weight, and capacity using measurement terms such as *shorter, longer, lighter, heavier, more than,* and *less than.*				X
Indicate an appropriate tool for the quantity or object being measured.				
Demonstrate an understanding of the concept of time, including use of the terms: *before, after, winter, summer, spring, autumn* or *fall, day, night, now,* and *tomorrow.*	X	X	X	X
Sort and match coins, face up and face down.				
SPATIAL RELATIONSHIPS AND TERMINOLOGY				
Identify relative positions using appropriate terminology.	X	X	X	X
OPERATION AND PLACE VALUE				
Use concrete objects to form addition sentences and demonstrate an understanding of the operation.				
Use concrete objects to answer subtraction questions and demonstrate an understanding of the operation.				
Respond to teacher-modeled questions and situations that involve addition of whole numbers using objects, pictures, or symbols.				
CHARTS AND GRAPHS				
Collect data by sorting counters using visual clues.				
Use information on a graph to analyze data and answer questions.				

Scope and Sequence Guidelines Time Line (Spanning Ten Months)						Evaluation and Support	
						Assessment Tool Page	Send-Home Card Page
5	6	7	8	9	10		
X	X	X	X	X	X	111	156, 157
		X	X	X	X	113	156
X	X	X	X	X	X	115	156
		X	X	X	X	117	158
X	X	X	X	X	X	119	159
			X	X	X	121	160
			X	X	X	121	160
			X	X	X	124	160
X	X	X	X	X	X	126	160, 161
X	X	X	X	X	X	126	160, 161

What Else Kids Need to Know

Although it is wide-ranging and features assessment guidelines and tools to help you evaluate a child's mastery of key areas within a typical pre-kindergarten curriculum, this book does not contain assessment information regarding every area of math mastery that can or should be assessed. To help you ascertain what further skill areas need to be assessed throughout the school year, refer to your state's standards and school district's curriculum and consider the skill lists provided below.

By the end of the school year, a pre-kindergartner should begin to . . .

Number Sense and Numeration

❏ Develop both ordinal and cardinal number concepts using naturally occurring opportunities (e.g., *How many pencils do we need? Who is third in line?*).

❏ Count with understanding and recognize "how many" in sets of objects 0–10 (e.g., dots on dominoes).

❏ Recognize when things are divided into equal parts through informal experiences with simple fractions.

❏ Begin to develop an understanding of the concepts of multiplication and division by using real objects to solve story problems involving repeated joining (addition) of groups of equal size or distribution of equal shares.

❏ Understand that sometimes you can estimate the number of objects in a set of 10 or less, and learn to recognize when an estimate is reasonable.

❏ Develop a sense of whole numbers and represent them in flexible ways.

Algebra

❏ Find and explore patterns in real life and understand that patterns can help us predict what comes next (e.g., explore repeating and growing patterns in rhythmic chants, repetitive songs, predictive poems, clapping patterns, clothing, and nature).

❏ Repeat, create, and extend number patterns. Count by 5s to 30 and 10s to 100.

❏ Count backwards 10–1.

❏ Use concrete, pictorial, and verbal representations to develop an understanding of the symbols used in mathematics. (e.g., A child may say "3 + 2 is 5 and 2 more is 7.")

❏ Model situations that involve addition and subtraction of whole numbers. Use familiar objects, pictures, and symbols (e.g., There are four children. Each of the children wants to eat two cookies. How many cookies do we need all together?).

❏ Describe qualitative change, such as hair growing longer.

❏ Describe quantitative change, such as a child growing two inches in one year.

Geometry

❏ Recognize describe, name, build, draw, manipulate, and sort two- and three-dimensional solid shapes (including the basic shapes on page 92, the sphere, cone, cube, and rectangular and triangular prisms).

❏ Begin to explore and investigate attributes of shapes (e.g., Take apart a cereal box, experiment with folded paper, create shapes on geoboards or dot paper, and so on).

❏ Mark a path to make a simple map and begin to distinguish navigation concepts, such as left and right.

❏ Solve puzzles using transformations, such as slides, flips, and turns.

❏ With teacher guidance, recognize, describe, and informally prove symmetric characteristics of design (e.g., use pattern blocks to create designs with line and rotational symmetry).

❏ Create mental images of geometric shapes using spatial memory and spatial visualization. (e.g., experiment with loops of string to make shapes).

❏ Exhibit enhanced visualization. Ask children to recall the number of dots on dominoes. Take visualization a step further by asking children to figure out the number of dots on a particular domino without counting. Remove an object from a group on the overhead (e.g., *What's missing?*).

❏ Recognize shapes from different perspectives.

❏ Begin to relate ideas in geometry to ideas in number and measurement (e.g., *It took 12 tiles to cover the area of this square.*).

Measurement

❏ Explore measurement through play.

❏ Measure using non-standard and standard units and understand the difference between them (e.g., measure with paper clips laid end to end; measure the length of a table with a tape measure).

Data Analysis and Probability

❏ Use informal sorting experiences in order to focus attention on common attributes (e.g., sorting groceries).

❏ Use simple grids to play games (i.e., bingo, tic-tac-toe) and to read a calendar.

❏ Understand that we can make predictions or decisions based on data we have collected from past experiences or class discussions.

❏ Begin to use the simple language of probability (e.g., *might, probably*).

❏ Discuss events related to the child's experiences as likely or unlikely.

❏ Ask questions, collect data, and record the results using objects, pictures, and picture graphs.

Problem Solving

❏ Solve problems related to daily routines or as a response to mathematical situations identified in a story.

❏ Solve problems that relate to classification, shape, or space (e.g., *Which blocks will fit on the shelf? Which blocks do you need to model a giraffe? Home many figures are alike and how many are different? Will this puzzle piece fit in the space that remains?*).

Reasoning and Proof

❏ Make decisions about how to solve a problem.

❏ Determine the approach, materials, and strategies to be used.

❏ Use pictorial representations or concrete objects to explain the reasoning used to solve problems.

❏ Manipulate common objects, identify how they are alike or different, and state generalizations about them.

❏ Use mathematical vocabulary to help verify or disprove conjectures.

Communication

❏ Communicate using mathematical terminology (e.g., *more* milk, *three* books, a *different* toy).

❏ Talk about mathematics, explain answers, and describe strategies. You can help children develop metacognitive skills by having them "reflect on" or "think about their thinking."

❏ Listen attentively to each other, question each other's strategies and results, and ask for clarification so that each child's mathematical learning advances.

Connections

❏ Connect the intuitive, informal mathematics that children have learned through their own experiences with the mathematics studied at school (e.g., A pre-kindergartner might hold up four fingers and ask, "Am I this many years old?," to connect the word four and the number it represents). You can help children make these connections by encouraging this informal math talk.

❏ Use mathematics in daily activities (e.g., counting syllables, counting the number of times a ball bounces in the gym, measuring for a recipe).

❏ Have experience answering teacher-directed questions that direct his or her thinking and present tasks that help the child to see how ideas are related.

Representation

❏ Use natural language, manipulatives (e.g., his or her own fingers), physical gestures, drawings, and symbols to represent an understanding of mathematical ideas.

Shapes

Properties and Relationships

DIRECTIONS

1. Explain to the child that he or she will be looking at shapes that he or she might recognize.

2. Point to the first shape in the row and ask the child to identify it.

3. Write a checkmark on the Teacher Form if the child identifies the shape correctly. If child makes an error, record the child's response.

4. Have the child describe the shape in his or her own words. You might say, "Tell me about this shape. How it is similar or different from other shapes on this page?"

5. Ask the child to name one familiar item that has the same shape. Invite the child to look around the room for examples.

6. Repeat the process of having the child identify one shape at a time until he or she has attempted to identify all of the shapes and provided two examples for each.

ASSESSMENT OBJECTIVES

The child can:

❒ Recognize and identify simple two-dimensional geometric shapes (e.g., circle, square, oval, triangle, and rectangle)

❒ Compare and describe geometric shapes using common attributes (straight lines, roundedness, number of corners, number of sides)

❒ Recognize and identify geometric shapes and structures in the environment

MATERIALS

• two blank sheets of paper (for masking)

• a copy of this form and the Student Form (page 92) for use with each child

---

TEACHER FORM

	Child's Response	Child's Description	Child's Examples
Circle			
Square			
Oval			
Triangle			
Rectangle			

Notes

CHILD'S NAME

DATE

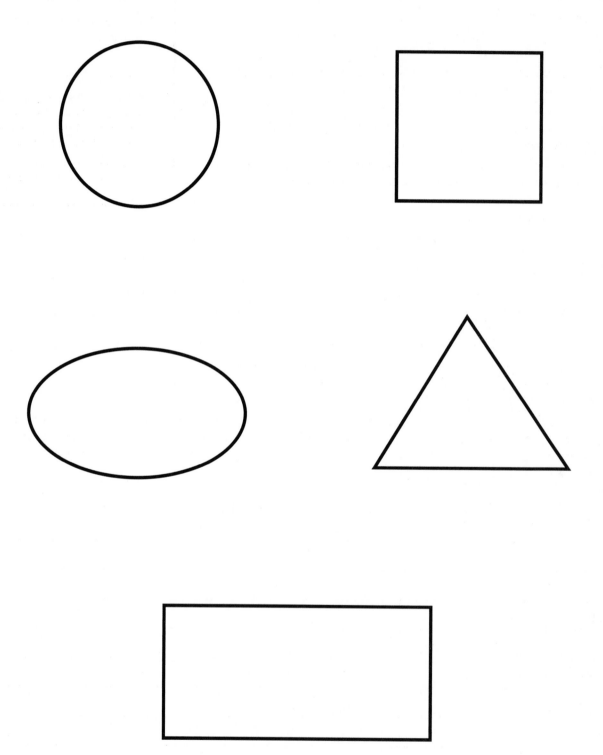

Numeration

Recognizing Numerals

ASSESSMENT OBJECTIVES

The child can:

❑ Recognize and identify the numerals from 0–9

❑ Rote count by ones from 1–10 or higher

MATERIALS

• two blank sheets of paper (for masking) and a copy of the Teacher Form (this page and page 94) for use with each child

• a copy of the Student Form (page 95) for each child

DIRECTIONS

Part A

1. Explain to the child that he or she will be identifying familiar numerals.

2. Point to the first numeral in the row of the Student Form and ask the child to identify the numeral.

3. Write a checkmark on the Teacher Form if the child identifies the numeral correctly. If the child makes an error, record the child's response.

4. Repeat the process of having the child name a numeral until he or she has attempted to identify all the numerals on the form.

Part B

5. Explain to the child that he or she should count aloud as high as he or she can, beginning with the number 1.

6. Use the number line on the Teacher Form as a place to record the child's counting behaviors. For each number he or she says in sequence, write a checkmark. Circle each number the child omits or repeats, unless the child corrects him- or herself.

7. Record the number to which the child counts and the date of the assessment.

TEACHER FORM

Part A: Identifying Numerals

Numeral	1st Assessment Child's Response	2nd Assessment Child's Response	3rd Assessment Child's Response	4th Assessment Child's Response
0				
1				
2				
3				
4				
5				
6				
7				
8				
9				
	Date _____ Score ____ /10	Date _____ Score ____ /10	Date _____ Score ____ /10	Date _____ Score ____ /10

CHILD'S NAME

Part B: Counting from 1 to 10 or higher.

1st Assessment

1   2   3   4   5   6   7   8   9   10

Counts to _____   Date _____

2nd Assessment

1   2   3   4   5   6   7   8   9   10

Counts to _____   Date _____

3rd Assessment

1   2   3   4   5   6   7   8   9   10

Counts to _____   Date _____

4th Assessment

1   2   3   4   5   6   7   8   9   10

Counts to _____   Date _____

Notes

Part A: I can identify numerals.

5   4

1   7   9

3   8

6   2   0

CHILD'S NAME

DATE

Numeration

Quantity and Correspondence

DIRECTIONS

1. Explain to the child that he or she will be counting to show "how many."

2. Read aloud to the child the numeral printed at the beginning of the row on the Student Form. Ask the child to count aloud the number words while he or she uses a pencil to mark how many objects that numeral represents. (Advise the child to simply mark the objects or draw a line through them, rather than coloring the objects.)

3. Repeat the process of having the child count and mark the quantity indicated by the numeral on the form.

4. Optional: If the child is ready, invite him or her to read the numeral and count the objects independently.

ASSESSMENT OBJECTIVES

The child can:

❏ Count objects to match the numerals 0–10

❏ Establish a one-to-one correspondence by marking objects while saying aloud the number word

MATERIALS

• pencils, two blank sheets of paper (for masking), and a copy of this page for use with each child

• a copy of the Student Form (page 97) for each child

TEACHER FORM

Answer Key

4	
3	
2	
10	
5	
8	
6	
9	
7	
1	
0	

1st Assessment	2nd Assessment	3rd Assessment	4th Assessment
Date _____	Date _____	Date _____	Date _____
Score ____ /10	Score ____ /10	Score ____ /10	Score ____ /10

Record your notes on the back of this page.

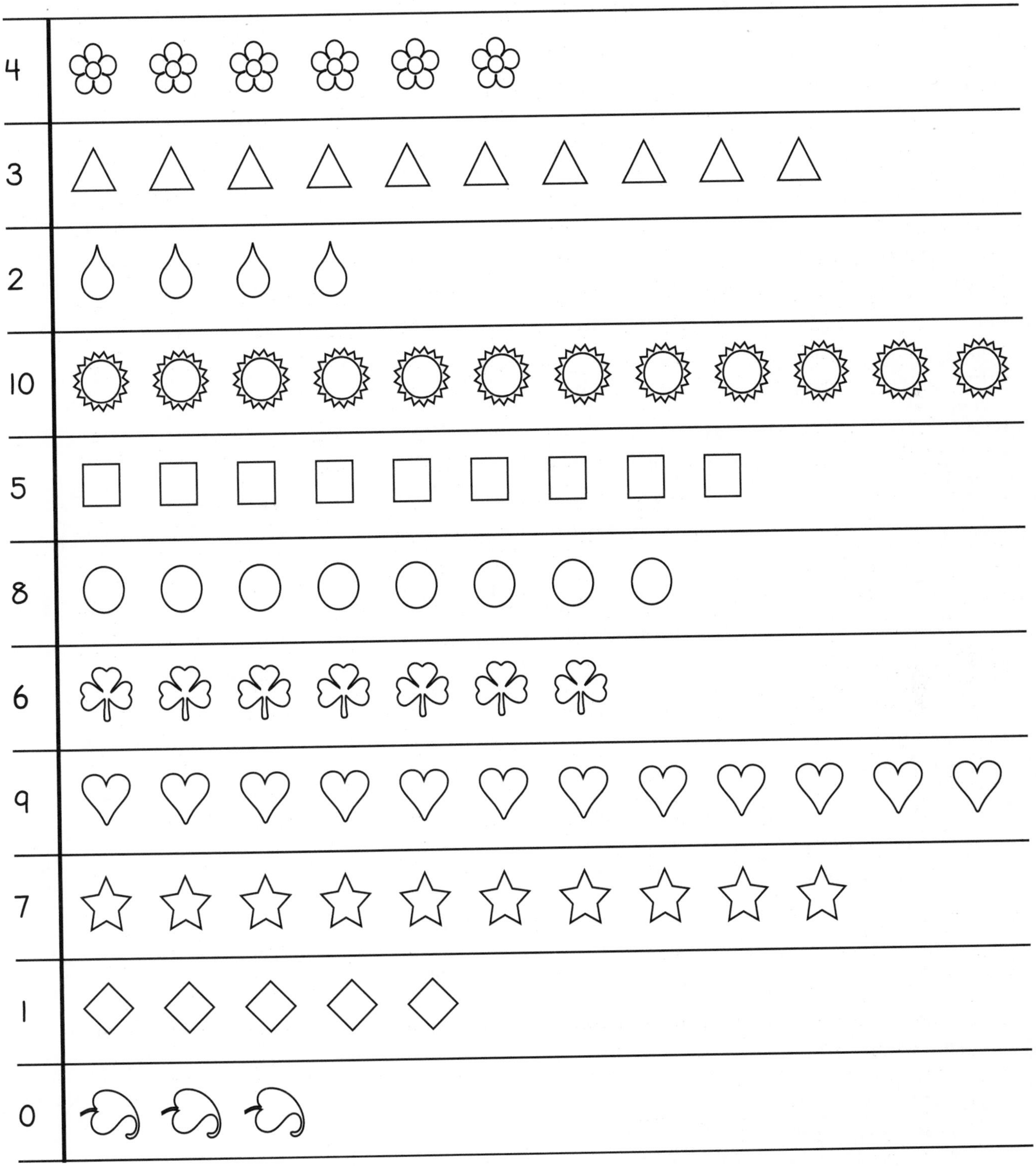

4	🌼 🌼 🌼 🌼 🌼 🌼
3	△ △ △ △ △ △ △ △ △ △
2	◊ ◊ ◊ ◊
10	☀ ☀ ☀ ☀ ☀ ☀ ☀ ☀ ☀ ☀ ☀ ☀
5	□ □ □ □ □ □ □ □ □
8	○ ○ ○ ○ ○ ○ ○ ○
6	☘ ☘ ☘ ☘ ☘ ☘ ☘
9	♡ ♡ ♡ ♡ ♡ ♡ ♡ ♡ ♡ ♡ ♡ ♡
7	☆ ☆ ☆ ☆ ☆ ☆ ☆ ☆ ☆ ☆
1	◇ ◇ ◇ ◇ ◇
0	🍎 🍎 🍎

CHILD'S NAME

DATE

Easy Assessments for Pre-Kindergarten © 2007 Laurie B. Fyke, Scholastic Teaching Resources

Numeration

Comparing Sets by Number

DIRECTIONS

1. Display three sheets of construction paper side by side on a flat surface in front of the child.

2. Explain that you will show three sets of objects, one set per sheet of colored paper. The child should look at the sets and then answer your questions.

3. Record a checkmark on the Teacher Form, if the child answers correctly. If the child makes an error, record his or her response.

Part A

4. Assemble the first three sets of objects, with no more than five objects in each grouping (see your Teacher Form for guidance).

5. Tell the child to indicate which set has a quantity . . .

- **equal to another set.** Then ask the child to explain his or her answer. You might say, "Point to the two sets that contain the same number of objects." (Child points to two sets.) You might ask, "Why did you pick those two?"

- **more than another set.** Then ask the child to explain his or her answer. You might say, "Point to the set that contains the most or more objects than the others." (Child points to a set.) You might ask, "Why did you pick that one?"

- **less than another set.** Then ask the child to explain his or her answer. You might say, "Point to the set that contains fewer objects than the others." (Child points to a set.) You might ask, "Why did you pick that one?"

Part B

6. Explain that now you will give the child an opportunity to make sets of his or her own.

7. Tell the child to place . . .

- **the same quantity of objects in two of the three groups.** Ask the child to indicate which two sets have the same quantity. Then ask the child to explain his or her answer. You might say, "Point to the two sets that contain the same number of objects." (Child points to two sets.) You might ask, "Why did you pick those two?"

- **a different quantity of objects in each group.** Ask the child to indicate which set has more than another set. Then ask the child to explain his or her answer. You might say, "Point to the set that contains the most or more objects than the others." (Child points to a set.) You might ask, "Why did you pick that one?"

- **a quantity less than another set.** Then ask the child to explain his or her answer. You might say, "Point to the set that contains fewer objects than the others." (Child points to a set.) You might ask, "Why did you pick that one?"

ASSESSMENT OBJECTIVES

The child can:

❒ Compare and identify sets that contain up to five objects (*more than, less than, equal to*)

MATERIALS

- three sheets of construction paper (of different colors), and a copy of this page and the Teacher Form (page 99) for use with each child

- three sets of five math manipulatives that can be used as counters (Ideally the manipulatives in each set are the same size and color. Items such as bingo chips, beans, and checkers game pieces work well for this activity.)

NUMERATION: COMPARING SETS BY NUMBER

	1st Assessment Child's Response	2nd Assessment Child's Response	3rd Assessment Child's Response	4th Assessment Child's Response
Part A: Sets Made by Teacher				
Equal To: Display one group of 3 objects, one group of 2 objects, and another group of 3 objects.				
More Than: Display one group of 2 objects, one group of 5 objects, and another group of 0 objects.				
Less Than: Display one group of 3 objects, one group of 4 objects, and another group of 1 object.				
Part B: Sets Made by Child				
Equal To: Display two groups of the same quantity.				
More Than: Display three groups of different quantities.				
Less Than: Display one group with fewer objects than another.				
	Date _____ Score ____ /6	Date _____ Score ____ /6	Date _____ Score ____ /6	Date _____ Score ____ /6

CHILD'S NAME

Answer Key

Part A: Comparisons of Sets Made by Teacher

Equal To: The two sets of three objects have quantities that are equal.

More Than: The set of five objects has the most.

Less Than: The set of one object has the fewest.

Part B: Comparisons of Sets Made by Child

Equal To: Answers will vary.

More Than: Answers will vary.

Less Than: Answers will vary.

Record your notes on the back of this page.

Comparing Sets by Attributes

DIRECTIONS

1. Display the two sheets of construction paper side by side on a flat surface in front of the child. In the same work area, display the collection of manipulatives.
2. Explain to the child that he or she will be using the shapes in the collection to form two sets.
3. Tell the child to form two sets. Explain that the child does not need to use all the shapes in the collection to make the two sets. He or she need only to place in each set the shapes that share an attribute or "go together."
4. When the child has finished sorting, ask him or her to explain how he or she sorted. You might ask, "Why did you place those shapes in two different sets?"
5. If the child sorted correctly, note what common attribute the child sorted by and record a checkmark on your Teacher Form. If the child makes an error, record his or her response.
6. Repeat the process of having the child sort and explain his or her reasoning four more times.

ASSESSMENT OBJECTIVES

The child can:

❑ Sort, classify, and order sets according to the attributes of shape, size, and color

MATERIALS

- two sheets of construction paper (of the same color), and a copy of this page and page 101 for use with each child
- a collection of manipulatives in a variety of geometric shapes, sizes, and colors (Simply precut construction paper or craft foam sheets into approximately twenty shapes that vary in size and color: circles, squares, triangles, rectangles)

TEACHER FORM

1st Assessment

Sets Made by Child	Child's Response	Notes
Common Attribute:		
Common Attribute:		
Common Attribute:		
Common Attribute:		
Common Attribute:		
	Date _____ Score ____ /5	

ORDERING AND SORTING: COMPARING SETS BY ATTRIBUTES

2nd Assessment

Sets Made by Child	Child's Response	Notes
Common Attribute:		
Common Attribute:		
Common Attribute:		
Common Attribute:		
Common Attribute:		
	Date _____ Score ____ /5	

3rd Assessment

Sets Made by Child	Child's Response	Notes
Common Attribute:		
Common Attribute:		
Common Attribute:		
Common Attribute:		
Common Attribute:		
	Date _____ Score ____ /5	

4th Assessment

Sets Made by Child	Child's Response	Notes
Common Attribute:		
Common Attribute:		
Common Attribute:		
Common Attribute:		
Common Attribute:		
	Date _____ Score ____ /5	

CHILD'S NAME

Ordering and Sorting

Smallest to Largest

ASSESSMENT OBJECTIVES

The child can:

❏ Order objects according to size

MATERIALS

• a set of picture cards (made from the Teacher Form on page 103) and a copy of this page for use with each child

DIRECTIONS

1. Show the picture cards to the child and ask him or her to examine them. Explain that he or she should sort the picture cards according to your directions.

2. Tell the child to sort the objects shown on the picture cards according to size, from smallest to largest.

3. If the child's sorting behavior demonstrates understanding, circle "yes" in the assessment grid below. If the child makes errors, circle "no" in the grid.

TEACHER FORM

Was the child able to order the cards from smallest to largest?

1st Assessment	2nd Assessment	3rd Assessment	4th Assessment
YES NO	YES NO	YES NO	YES NO
Date _____	Date _____	Date _____	Date _____

Notes

Answer Key

Smallest

Largest

DIRECTIONS

Copy this page and laminate it for durability. Cut out the cards along the dashed lines. Store them in a sturdy envelope or self-sealing bag.

Ordering and Sorting

Three Stages of Development

ASSESSMENT OBJECTIVES

The child can:

❐ Sequence three stages of development

DIRECTIONS

1. Show the picture cards to the child and ask him or her to examine them. Explain that he or she should sort the picture cards according to your directions.

2. Instruct the child to sort the picture cards according to the order in which they might happen, in sequence from earliest to latest.

3. If the child's sorting behavior demonstrates understanding, circle "yes" in the assessment grid below. If the child makes errors, circle "no" in the grid.

MATERIALS

• a set of picture cards (made from the Teacher Form on page 105) and a copy of this page for use with each child

TEACHER FORM

Was the child able to order the cards in sequence from earliest to latest?

1st Assessment	2nd Assessment	3rd Assessment	4th Assessment
YES NO	YES NO	YES NO	YES NO
Date _____	Date _____	Date _____	Date _____

Notes

Answer Key

Earliest   Latest

DIRECTIONS

Copy this page and laminate it for durability. Cut out the cards along the dashed lines. Store them in a sturdy envelope or self-sealing bag.

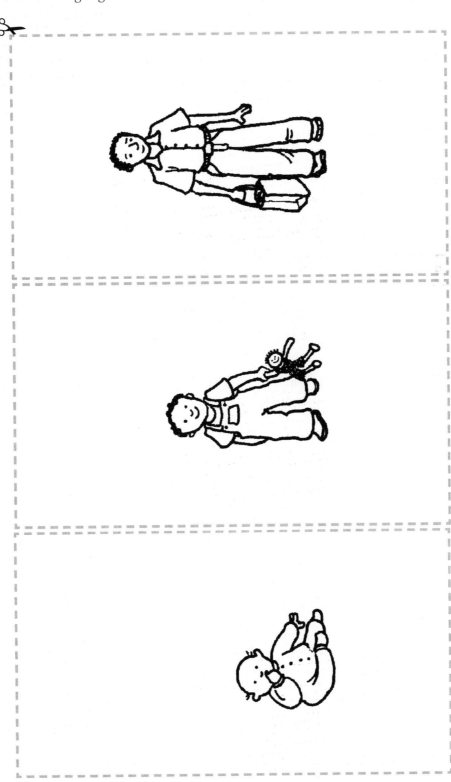

Ordering and Sorting

Comparing Opposites

ASSESSMENT OBJECTIVES

The child can:

❏ Compare pictures of objects using knowledge of opposites

MATERIALS

• a set of picture cards (made from the Teacher Form on page 107) and a copy of this page for use with each child

DIRECTIONS

1. Review the concept of opposite.
2. Show the picture cards to the child and ask him or her to examine them. Explain that he or she will find the opposite of the card you choose.
3. Point to the "cold" card and say, "Show me the opposite of cold."
4. Repeat this procedure for the rest of the pairs.
5. If the child's sorting behavior demonstrates understanding, circle "yes" in the assessment grid below (See Answer Key). If the child makes errors, circle "no" in the grid.

TEACHER FORM

Was the child able to order sort the cards in pairs to show opposites?

Answer Key		1st Assessment	2nd Assessment	3rd Assessment	4th Assessment
cold	*hot*	YES NO	YES NO	YES NO	YES NO
awake	*asleep*	YES NO	YES NO	YES NO	YES NO
light	*heavy*	YES NO	YES NO	YES NO	YES NO
full	*empty*	YES NO	YES NO	YES NO	YES NO
long	*short*	YES NO	YES NO	YES NO	YES NO
		Date _____	Date _____	Date _____	Date _____

Answer Key

Children should pair: *cold* with *hot*, *awake* with *asleep*, *light* with *heavy*, *full* with *empty*, and *long* with *short*.

Record your notes on the back of this page.

ORDERING AND SORTING: COMPARING OPPOSITES

DIRECTIONS

Copy this page and laminate it for durability. Cut out the cards along the dashed lines. Store them in a sturdy envelope or self-sealing bag.

Ordering and Sorting

Simple Patterns

DIRECTIONS

1. Explain to the child that he or she will be working with patterns.
2. Distribute the Student Form and the set of patterns cards to the child.
3. Point to the first pattern on the Student Form and point out that the sequence is not complete.
4. Explain to the child that he or she should place the pattern cards on the Student Form to copy and complete the pattern.
5. Tell the child to say aloud the completed pattern. (Note: If the child corrects him- or herself when telling the pattern aloud, accept the correction and record your observation below.)
6. Repeat the process of having the child examine the pattern, copy and complete the pattern, and identify the pattern aloud until the child has attempted to complete the first three patterns.
7. Point to the fourth row on the Student Form. Explain that you, the teacher, will use that row to create a pattern using the pattern cards.
8. Tell the child to use pattern cards to copy and repeat the pattern. As before, tell the child to say the pattern aloud.

ASSESSMENT OBJECTIVES

The child can:

❏ Identify, copy, and repeat simple patterns (e.g., ab, abc, aabb)

MATERIALS

• crayons, a set of pattern cards (made from the Teacher Form on page 109), a laminated copy of the Student Form (page 110), and a copy of this page for use with each child

TEACHER FORM

Was the child able to identify and extend simple patterns?

1st Assessment	2nd Assessment	3rd Assessment	4th Assessment
YES NO	YES NO	YES NO	YES NO
Date _____	Date _____	Date _____	Date _____

Answer Key

Row 1: star, circle, star, circle, star, circle, star, circle, <u>star</u>, <u>circle</u>

Row 2: triangle, heart, star, triangle, heart, star, triangle, heart, <u>star</u>, <u>triangle</u>

Row 3: circle, triangle, circle, triangle, <u>circle</u>, <u>triangle</u>, <u>circle</u>, <u>triangle</u>, <u>circle</u>, <u>triangle</u>

Row 4: Child should use the pattern cards to extend a pattern at his or her level of difficulty.

Record your notes on the back of this page.

DIRECTIONS

Copy this page and laminate it for durability. Cut out the cards along the dashed lines. Store them in a sturdy envelope or self-sealing bag.

Row 4 | Row 3 | Row 2 | Row 1

Measurement, Time, and Money

Comparing Length, Weight, and Capacity

ASSESSMENT OBJECTIVES

The child can:

❐ Compare length, weight, and capacity using measurement terms such as shorter, longer, lighter, heavier, more than, and less than

MATERIALS

• a set of measurement cards (made from the Teacher Form on page 112) and a copy of this page for use with each child

DIRECTIONS

1. Explain that you will show the child pairs of pictures and then ask a question. Explain that he or she should look carefully at each picture before answering.

2. Select two picture cards labeled *length* and show them to the child. (Note: If you need to repeat this assessment later in the year, select cards that are unfamiliar to the child.)

3. Tell the child to indicate which picture shows an object a) that is shorter and b) that is longer than the other. Ask the child to explain his or her answers (see Answer Key).

4. If the child's response demonstrates understanding, circle "yes" in the grid below (See Answer Key). If the child makes errors, circle "no" in the grid below.

5. Select two picture cards labeled *weight* and continue the process as above, this time asking the child to indicate which picture shows an object a) that is lighter and b) that is heavier in weight than the other.

6. Select two picture cards labeled *capacity* and continue the process as above, this time asking the child to indicate which picture shows a container that can a) hold less and b) hold more than the other.

TEACHER FORM

Type of Measurement	1st Assessment	2nd Assessment	3rd Assessment	4th Assessment
Was the child able to compare pictured objects in relation to length?	YES NO	YES NO	YES NO	YES NO
Was the child able to compare pictured objects in relation to weight?	YES NO	YES NO	YES NO	YES NO
Was the child able to compare pictured objects in relation to capacity?	YES NO	YES NO	YES NO	YES NO
	Date _____	Date _____	Date _____	Date _____

CHILD'S NAME

Answer Key
Length: Students should indicate that the nail is shorter than the screwdriver, the screwdriver is shorter than the pliers, and the pliers are shorter than the wrench. Longer: (relationships mentioned in reverse).

Weight: Students should indicate that the tooth weighs less than the mouse, the mouse weighs less than the backpack, and the backpack weighs less than the car. Heavier: (relationships mentioned in reverse).

Capacity: Students should indicate that the baby bottle holds more than the dropper, the bucket holds more than the baby bottle, and the bathtub holds more than the bucket. More: (relationships mentioned in reverse).

Record your notes on the back of this page.

DIRECTIONS

Copy this page and laminate it for durability. Cut out the cards along the dashed lines. Store them in a sturdy envelope or self-sealing bag.

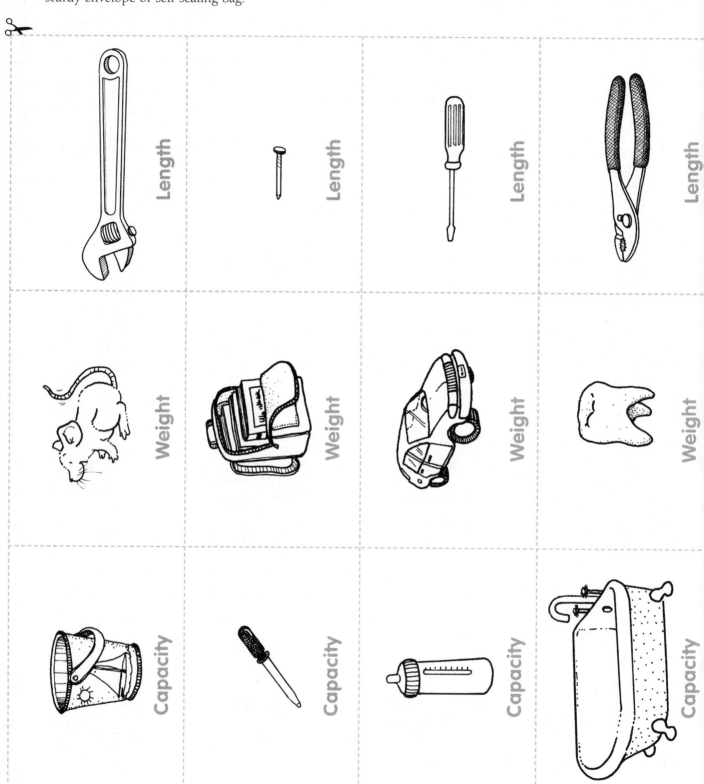

Measurement, Time, and Money

Matching Tools and Traits

ASSESSMENT OBJECTIVES

The child can:

❐ Indicate an appropriate tool for the quantity or object being measured

MATERIALS

• a laminated copy of the Student Form (page 114) and a copy of this page for use with each child

DIRECTIONS

1. Familiarize yourself with the ten questions on the Teacher Form below.

2. Show the child the illustrations on the Student Form and explain that different tools help measure different quantities. Tell the child that you will be asking several questions about measuring, and he or she should indicate which pictured tool would best be used to answer each question, in turn.

3. Ask the first question on the Teacher Form below and wait for the child's response. (You might use the prompt that begins "Which tool should you use to find out . . ." and then specify the quantity indicated.)

4. Write a checkmark on the Teacher Form if the child responds correctly. If the child makes an error, record the error and your observations in the notes section. (Note: If a child appears to answer incorrectly, invite him or her to elaborate, as some measurements can be evaluated appropriately with more than one tool or with a tool not pictured on the Student Form. For example, to measure the weight of a brick, a child might select the bathroom scale or the balance.)

5. Repeat the process until the child has attempted to respond to all ten questions.

TEACHER FORM

Questions/Prompt: *Which tool should you use to find out . . . ?*	Child's Response			
	1st Assessment	**2nd Assessment**	**3rd Assessment**	**4th Assessment**
1. how much you weigh				
2. how many days until a holiday				
3. the time you go home				
4. how tall you are				
5. how much water for one drink				
6. how much salt to add to a recipe				
7. how long a bus is				
8. how cold it is outside				
9. how long your finger is				
10. if two blocks weigh the same				
	Date _____ Score ____ /10	Date _____ Score ____ /10	Date _____ Score ____ /10	Date _____ Score ____ /10

CHILD'S NAME

Answer Key

1. scale **2.** calendar **3.** clock **4.** measuring tape **5.** measuring cup **6.** measuring spoon
7. measuring tape **8.** thermometer **9.** ruler **10.** balance

Record your notes on the back of this page.

DIRECTIONS

Copy this page and laminate it for durability.

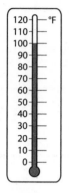

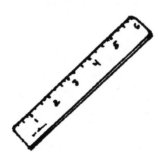

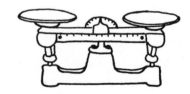

Measurement, Time, and Money

Using Time Vocabulary

DIRECTIONS

1. Explain to the child that you will be asking questions about pairs of pictures.

2. Show the first pair and ask the child to answer questions involving the concepts of *before* and *after*. You might say, "Which would you more likely see first? [Pause for response.] And after?"

3. If the child's explanation demonstrates understanding, record a checkmark in the assessment grid below. If child makes errors, record your observations in the notes section.

4. Repeat the process until the child has examined all of the picture pairs and attempted to respond to all of the concept-related questions. For picture pairs two through five, you might use prompts such as these:
Pair Two: winter/summer: "Which would you more likely see in the winter? [Pause for response.] In the summer?"
Pair Three: autumn/spring: "Which would you more likely see in the springtime? [Pause for response.] In the autumn or fall?"
Pair Four: day/night: "Which would you more likely see during the daytime? [Pause for response.] In the nighttime?"
Pair Five: now/tomorrow: "Which would help you figure out what day tomorrow will be? [Pause for response.] Which would help you figure out what time it is right now?"

ASSESSMENT OBJECTIVES

The child can:

❒ Demonstrate an understanding of the concept of time, including use of the terms: *before, after, winter, summer, spring, autumn* or *fall, day, night, now,* and *tomorrow*

MATERIALS

• two blank sheets of paper (for masking), a copy of the the Student Form (on page 116), and a copy of this page for use with each child

TEACHER FORM

Picture Pairs	1st Assessment	2nd Assessment	3rd Assessment	4th Assessment
before/after				
winter/summer				
spring/autumn				
day/night				
now/tomorrow				
	Date _____ Score ____ /10	Date _____ Score ____ /10	Date _____ Score ____ /10	Date _____ Score ____ /10

CHILD'S NAME

Notes

DIRECTIONS

Copy this page and laminate it for durability.

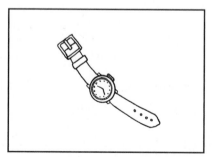

Measurement, Time, and Money

Sorting and Matching Coins

ASSESSMENT OBJECTIVES

The child can:

❐ Sort and match coins, face up and facedown

MATERIALS

- two blank sheets of paper (for masking) and a laminated copy of the Student Form (page 118)
- a copy of this page for use with each child
- two of each coin pictured on the Student Form

DIRECTIONS

1. Set out the eight coins so that each is shown face up and facedown. Set out the Student Form.
2. Ask the child to match the coins to the pictures by placing them on top of the correct picture on the Student Form.
3. To begin, ask the child to put the pennies on the matching pictures. If the child indicates that he or she sees just one penny, you might say: "Pennies have two sides. Show me a picture of another coin that might also be a penny."
4. Mark the corresponding coins pictured on the Teacher Form with checkmarks if the child sorts and matches the coins correctly. If the child makes an error, record his or her response. If the child finds the task too difficult overall, stop testing.
5. Repeat the process until the child has sorted and matched the face up and facedown versions of all the coins on the Student Form (pennies, nickels, dimes, quarters).

TEACHER FORM

1st Assessment

Date _____   Score _____ /8

2nd Assessment

Date _____   Score _____ /8

3rd Assessment

Date _____   Score _____ /8

4th Assessment

Date _____   Score _____ /8

Record your notes on the back of this page.

CHILD'S NAME

DIRECTIONS

Copy this page and laminate it for durability.

Spatial Relationships and Terminology

Relative Positions

ASSESSMENT OBJECTIVES

The child can:
- ❏ Identify relative positions using appropriate terminology

MATERIALS
- two blank sheets of paper (for masking), a copy of the Student Form (on page 120) and a copy of this page for use with each child

DIRECTIONS

1. Explain to the child that you will be asking questions about where things are located.
2. To begin, tell the child to examine the Student Form. Ask the child to identify the position of the objects pictured. You might use the prompts suggested on the Teacher Form.
3. Write a checkmark on the Teacher Form if the child demonstrates an understanding of the spatial relationship and the terminology. If the child makes an error, record the child's response.
4. Repeat the process until the child has identified all spatial relationships in the grid located on the Teacher Form.

TEACHER FORM

Position	Suggested Prompts	Child's Response			
		1st Assessment	2nd Assessment	3rd Assessment	4th Assessment
up/down	Show me the arrow that is pointing down.				
near/far	Show me the tree that is far away.				
in front of/ behind	Tell me about this picture. Point to the ball behind the dog.				
on top of/ beneath	Tell me about this picture. Point to the lamp that is under the desk.				
around	Use your finger to draw a circle around the dog.				
under	Use your finger to draw a line under the cat.				
above	Use your finger to draw a line above the bear.				
last	Point to the last animal in the row. (cat)				
second	Point to the second animal in the row. (mouse)				
first	Point to the first animal in the row. (bear)				
		Date _____ Score ____ /10	Date _____ Score ____ /10	Date _____ Score ____ /10	Date _____ Score ____ /10

Notes

CHILD'S NAME

DIRECTIONS

Copy this page and laminate it for durability.

Operation and Place Value

Math Stories

ASSESSMENT OBJECTIVES

The child can:

❑ Use concrete objects to form addition sentences and demonstrate an understanding of the operation

❑ Use concrete objects to answer subtraction questions and demonstrate an understanding of the operation

MATERIALS

• a copy of this page for each child, a copy of the Teacher Form (page 122), and a laminated copy of the Student Form (page 123)

• For this assessment you will need a set of five math manipulatives that can be used as counters. (Ideally the manipulatives are the same size and color. Items such as bingo chips, beans, and checkers game pieces work well for this activity.)

DIRECTIONS

Part A

1. Display manipulatives on a flat surface in front of the child. Explain that he or she will be using the manipulatives to create math stories about adding objects.

2. Provide an example (see below), talking aloud as you position two sets of manipulatives (such as beans) in the example box of the Student Form.
   • You might say, "I'm working with the number 3. Here is my story: *Two beans* [pause] *and one bean* [pause] *makes three beans.* [pause] Now it's your turn."

3. Indicate the first box on the Student Form and ask the child to tell you a math story in which two quantities add up to four.

4. Have the child explain his or her reasoning. If the child's explanation demonstrates understanding of addition, record a checkmark in the assessment grid on the Teacher Form. If not, record the child's response.

5. Repeat the process until the child has created addition math stories for each numeral on the Student Form.

Part B

6. Explain to the child that he or she will be now be answering math stories about taking away objects.

7. Provide an example, talking aloud as you position two sets of manipulatives (such as beans) in the example box of the Student Form.
   • You might say, "I'm working with the number 3. Here is my story: *Three beans* [pause] *take away one bean* [pause and separate one bean from the others] *leaves two beans.* Now it's your turn."

8. Repeat the process, now with the child moving the manipulatives as you tell the story, until the child has answered subtraction stories for each numeral on the Student Form.

CHILD'S NAME

OPERATION AND PLACE VALUE: MATH STORIES

STUDENT FORM

DIRECTIONS

Copy this page and laminate it for durability.

I can create a math story.

example	
3	

OPERATION AND PLACE VALUE: MATH STORIES

Sample Assessment

	1st Assessment Child's Response	2nd Assessment Child's Response	3rd Assessment Child's Response	4th Assessment Child's Response
Part A: Addition *example: 3: 2 + 1*				
4	1 + 3 ✓			
5	2 + 3 ✓			
2	1 + 1 ✓			
Part B: Subtraction *example: 5 − 2 = 3*				
4	4 − 2 = 1			
5	5 − 1 = 2			
2	2 − 0 = 2 ✓			
	Date 10/2 Score 4 /6	Date ____ Score ____ /6	Date ____ Score ____ /6	Date ____ Score ____ /6

	1st Assessment Child's Response	2nd Assessment Child's Response	3rd Assessment Child's Response	4th Assessment Child's Response
Part A: Addition *example: 3: 2 + 1*				
4				
5				
2				
Part B: Subtraction *example: 5: 5 − 2 = 3*				
4				
5				
2				
	Date ____ Score ____ /6	Date ____ Score ____ /6	Date ____ Score ____ /6	Date ____ Score ____ /6

Answer Key

Part A: Addition

Students may say any one of the math sentences that follow.

4: 1 + 3, 2 + 2, 4 + 0

5: 1 + 4, 2 + 3, 5 + 0

2: 1 + 1, 2 + 0

Part B: Subtraction

Students may say any one of the math sentences that follow.

4: 4 − 0 = 4, 4 − 1 = 3, 4 − 2 = 2, 4 − 3, = 1, 4 − 4 = 0

5: 5 − 0 = 5, 5 − 1= 4, 5 − 2 = 3, 5 − 3 = 2, 5 − 4 = 1, 5 − 5 = 0

2: 2 − 0 = 2, 2 − 1 = 1, 2 − 2 = 0

Record your notes on the back of this page.

DIRECTIONS

Copy this page and laminate it for durability.

I can create a math story.

example	
3	
4	
5	
2	

MATHEMATICS

Operation and Place Value

Dictated Math Stories

DIRECTIONS

1. Explain to the child that you will be asking questions about "how many."
2. Point to the first box of the Student Form and ask the child to use his or her pencil to show the answer to your problem.
3. Ask, "If I had one snail and I found two more snails, how many snails would I have all together?" (The child should circle three snails.)
4. Record the child's solution in the first column of the Teacher Form. Write a checkmark in the assessment column if the child was able to solve the problem.
5. Repeat the process until the child has completed the form.

ASSESSMENT OBJECTIVES

The child can:

❏ Use pictorial models to demonstrate a developing understanding addition

MATERIALS

• a copy of the Student Form (page 125) for use with each child

TEACHER FORM

In each row, the child should circle the number of snails that represents the answer to your math story. Show his or her answer here.

	Child's Response			
	1st Assessment	2nd Assessment	3rd Assessment	4th Assessment
Row 1				
Row 2				
Row 3				
Row 4				
Row 5				
	Date _____	Date _____	Date _____	Date _____
	Score ____ /5	Score ____ /5	Score ____ /5	Score ____ /5

MATHEMATICS

I can solve a math problem.

CHILD'S NAME

DATE

Charts and Graphs

Collecting and Analyzing Data

DIRECTIONS

1. Explain to the child that he or she should sort the counters according to your directions (no more than six counters per group).

Part A

2. Have him or her sort the counters by common attributes, by how each type looks physically. To get the child started you might say "Put all the kidney beans in one group and all the green peas in another group."

3. If the child's sorting behavior demonstrates understanding, record a checkmark in the assessment grid (Part A). If he or she makes sorting errors, record your observations.

Part B

4. Give the Student Form to the child and demonstrate how he or she should place each group of counters (beans, in this example) in its own column in order to show how many beans there are of each kind.

5. After the child has completed the first row, point to the beans in the first column and tell the child to count the quantity aloud. Repeat a the process until he or she has placed and counted the beans in all three columns.

6. Ask the child to indicate which column has the most beans, which column has the fewest beans, and which columns have the same number of beans (if applicable). With each question about the graph, ask the child to explain his or her reasoning. If the child's explanation demonstrates understanding of the graph, record a checkmark in the assessment grid (Part B). If not, record the child's response.

ASSESSMENT OBJECTIVES

The child can:

❒ Collect data by sorting counters using visual cues (with regard to color, size, and shape)

❒ Use information on a graph to analyze data and answer questions

MATERIALS

- a laminated copy of the Student Form (on page 127) and a copy of this page for use with each child

- three sets of counters that can be used as math manipulatives (Each set should be comprised of items that are of the same size and color. Each set should contain a different quantity of counters than the others, with no more than six items in any set. All three sets of counters should be mixed in one container. Items such as dried kidney beans, lima beans, chickpeas, and green peas work well for this activity.)

TEACHER FORM

Part A : Collecting : Sorting by Color, Size, and Shape

1st Assessment	2nd Assessment	3rd Assessment	4th Assessment

Part B : Analyzing : Using Data From a Graph to Answer Questions

1st Assessment	2nd Assessment	3rd Assessment	4th Assessment
Date _____	Date _____	Date _____	Date _____

CHARTS AND GRAPHS: COLLECTING AND ANALYZING DATA

DIRECTIONS
Copy this page and laminate it for durability.

I can make a graph.

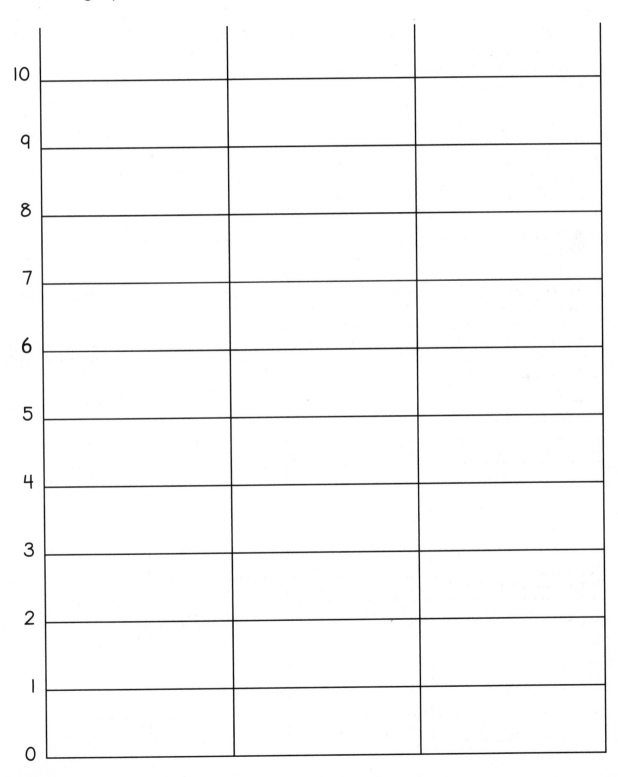

Record-Keeping Forms

STUDENT PROGRESS PROFILE: LANGUAGE ARTS

CHILD'S NAME _____

FOCUS	TOOL TITLE
Print Concepts	An Overview
Auditory Discrimination	Environmental Sounds
Visual Discrimination	Matching Pictures
	Word Sorting
	Matching Words
	Name Recognition
	Like Letters
Phonological Awareness	Syllables
	Segmentation of Sentences
	Perceiving Rhyme
	Making a Rhyme
	Blending Onsets and Rimes
	Letter Names
Phonemic Awareness	Letter Sounds
	Isolation of Sounds
	Matching Sounds
	Blending Phonemes
	Segmentation of Words
Reading	Read Original Writing
	Comprehension
Writing	Organizing Information
	Printing Familiar Letters
	Interactive and Shared Writing
	Risk Taking
	Communicating Ideas

Performance Level Key
Related skills appear to be: N = not yet appa...

130 *Easy Assessments for Pre-Kindergarten © 2007 Laura B. Pyke...*

STUDENT PROGRESS PROFILE: MATHEMATICS

CHILD'S NAME _____ YEAR _____ TEACHER _____

FOCUS	TOOL TITLE	PERFORMANCE LEVEL (Fill in letter code from key below.)			
		1st Assessment	2nd Assessment	3rd Assessment	4th Assessment
Shapes	Properties and Relationships				
Numeration	Recognizing Numerals				
	Quantity and Correspondence				
	Comparing Sets by Number				
Ordering and Sorting	Comparing Sets by Attributes				
	Smallest to Largest				
	Three Stages of Development				
	Comparing Opposites				
	Simple Patterns				
Measurement, Time, and Money	Comparing Length, Weight, and Capacity				
	Matching Tools and Traits				
	Using Time Vocabulary				
	Matching Coins				
Spatial Relationships and Terminology	Relative Positions				
Operation and Place Value	Math Stories				
	Dictated Math Stories				
Charts and Graphs	Collecting and Analyzing Data				

Performance Level Key
Related skills appear to be: N = not yet apparent   B = beginning to develop   D = developing
P = present   E = exceeding age expectations

WHOLE CLASS PROFILE: LANGUAGE ARTS

YEAR _____ TEACHER _____

FOCUS	TOOL TITLE
Print Concepts	An Overview
Auditory Discrimination	Environmental Sounds
Visual Discrimination	Matching Pictures
	Word Sorting
	Matching Words
	Name Recognition
	Like Letters
Phonological Awareness	Syllables
	Segmentation of Sentences
	Perceiving Rhyme
	Making a Rhyme
	Blending Onsets and Rimes
	Letter Names
Phonemic Awareness	Letter Sounds
	Isolation of Sounds
	Matching Sounds
	Blending Phonemes
	Segmentation of Words
Reading	Read Original Writing
	Comprehension
Writing	Organizing Information
	Printing Familiar Letters
	Inter...
	Risk ...
	Com...

Performance Level ...
Related skills appear to ...

132 *Easy Assessments for P...*

WHOLE CLASS PROFILE: MATHEMATICS

YEAR _____ TEACHER _____

FOCUS	TOOL TITLE
Shapes	Properties and Relationships
Numeration	Recognizing Numerals
	Printing Numerals
	Quantity and Correspondence
	Comparing Sets by Number
Ordering and Sorting	Comparing Sets by Attributes
	Smallest to Largest
	Three Stages of Development
	Comparing Opposites
	Simple Patterns
Measurement, Time, and Money	Comparing Length, Weight, and Capacity
	Matching Tools and Traits
	Using Time Vocabulary
	Matching Coins
Spatial Relationships and Terminology	Relative Positions
Operation and Place Value	Math Stories
	Dictated Math Stories
Charts and Graphs	Collecting and Analyzing Data

Performance Level Key
Related skills appear to be: N = not yet apparent   B = beginning to develop   D = developing
P = present   E = exceeding age expectations

134 *Easy Assessments for Pre-Kindergarten © 2007 Laura B. Pyke, Scholastic Teaching Resources*

135 *Easy Assessments for Pre-Kindergarten © 2007 Laura B. Pyke, Scholastic Teaching Resources*

STUDENT PROGRESS PROFILE: LANGUAGE ARTS

CHILD'S NAME _____ YEAR _____ TEACHER _____

FOCUS	TOOL TITLE	PERFORMANCE LEVEL (Fill in letter code from key below.)			
		1st Assessment	2nd Assessment	3rd Assessment	4th Assessment
Print Concepts	An Overview				
Auditory Discrimination	Environmental Sounds				
Visual Discrimination	Matching Pictures				
	Word Sorting				
	Matching Words				
	Name Recognition				
	Like Letters				
Phonological Awareness	Syllables				
	Segmentation of Sentences				
	Perceiving Rhyme				
	Making a Rhyme				
	Blending Onsets and Rimes				
	Letter Names				
Phonemic Awareness	Letter Sounds				
	Isolation of Sounds				
	Matching Sounds				
	Blending Phonemes				
	Segmentation of Words				
Reading	Read Original Writing				
	Comprehension				
Writing	Organizing Information				
	Printing Familiar Letters				
	Interactive and Shared Writing				
	Risk Taking				
	Communicating Ideas				

Performance Level Key

Related skills appear to be: **N** = not yet apparent   **B** = beginning to develop   **D** = developing
P = present   **E** = exceeding age expectations

Easy Assessments for Pre-Kindergarten © 2007 Laurie B. Fyke, Scholastic Teaching Resources

STUDENT PROGRESS PROFILE: MATHEMATICS

CHILD'S NAME _____ YEAR _____ TEACHER _____

FOCUS	TOOL TITLE	PERFORMANCE LEVEL (Fill in letter code from key below.)			
		1st Assessment	2nd Assessment	3rd Assessment	4th Assessment
Shapes	Properties and Relationships				
Numeration	Recognizing Numerals				
	Quantity and Correspondence				
	Comparing Sets by Number				
Ordering and Sorting	Comparing Sets by Attributes				
	Smallest to Largest				
	Three Stages of Development				
	Comparing Opposites				
	Simple Patterns				
Measurement, Time, and Money	Comparing Length, Weight, and Capacity				
	Matching Tools and Traits				
	Using Time Vocabulary				
	Matching Coins				
Spatial Relationships and Terminology	Relative Positions				
Operation and Place Value	Math Stories				
	Dictated Math Stories				
Charts and Graphs	Collecting and Analyzing Data				

Performance Level Key

Related skills appear to be: **N = not yet apparent   B = beginning to develop   D = developing**

P = present   E = exceeding age expectations

WHOLE CLASS PROFILE: LANGUAGE ARTS

YEAR _____ TEACHER _____

FOCUS	TOOL TITLE											
Print Concepts	An Overview											
Auditory Discrimination	Environmental Sounds											
Visual Discrimination	Matching Pictures											
	Word Sorting											
	Matching Words											
	Name Recognition											
	Like Letters											
Phonological Awareness	Syllables											
	Segmentation of Sentences											
	Perceiving Rhyme											
	Making a Rhyme											
	Blending Onsets and Rimes											
	Letter Names											
Phonemic Awareness	Letter Sounds											
	Isolation of Sounds											
	Matching Sounds											
	Blending Phonemes											
	Segmentation of Words											
Reading	Read Original Writing											
	Comprehension											
Writing	Organizing Information											
	Printing Familiar Letters											
	Interactive and Shared Writing											
	Risk Taking											
	Communicating Ideas											

Performance Level Key

Related skills appear to be: **N = not yet apparent   B = beginning to develop   D = developing**
P = present   E = exceeding age expectations

Easy Assessments for Pre-Kindergarten © 2007 Laurie B. Fyke, Scholastic Teaching Resources

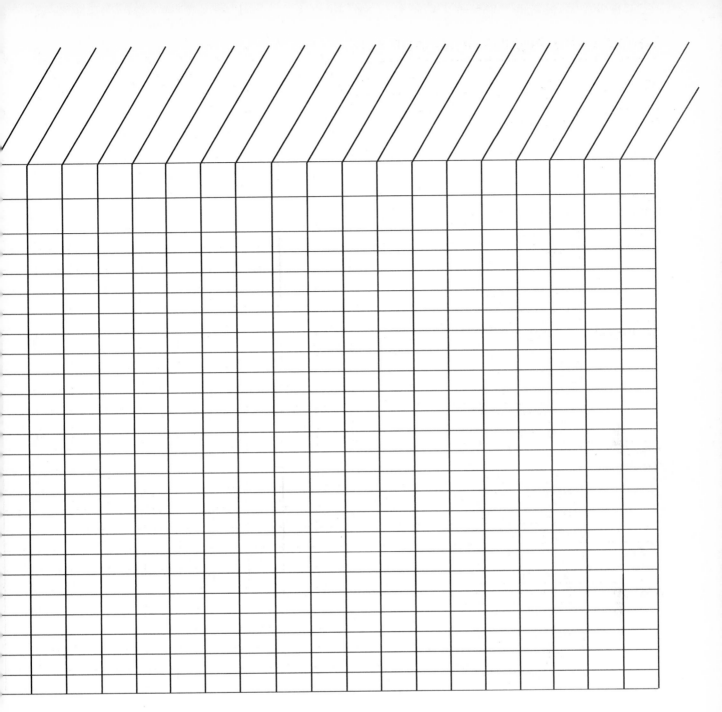

WHOLE CLASS PROFILE: MATHEMATICS

YEAR _____ TEACHER _____

FOCUS	TOOL TITLE											
Shapes	Properties and Relationships											
Numeration	Recognizing Numerals											
	Printing Numerals											
	Quantity and Correspondence											
	Comparing Sets by Number											
Ordering and Sorting	Comparing Sets by Attributes											
	Smallest to Largest											
	Three Stages of Development											
	Comparing Opposites											
	Simple Patterns											
Measurement, Time, and Money	Comparing Length, Weight, and Capacity											
	Matching Tools and Traits											
	Using Time Vocabulary											
	Matching Coins											
Spatial Relationships and Terminology	Relative Positions											
Operation and Place Value	Math Stories											
	Dictated Math Stories											
Charts and Graphs	Collecting and Analyzing Data											

Performance Level Key

Related skills appear to be: **N = not yet apparent   B = beginning to develop   D = developing**

P = present   E = exceeding age expectations

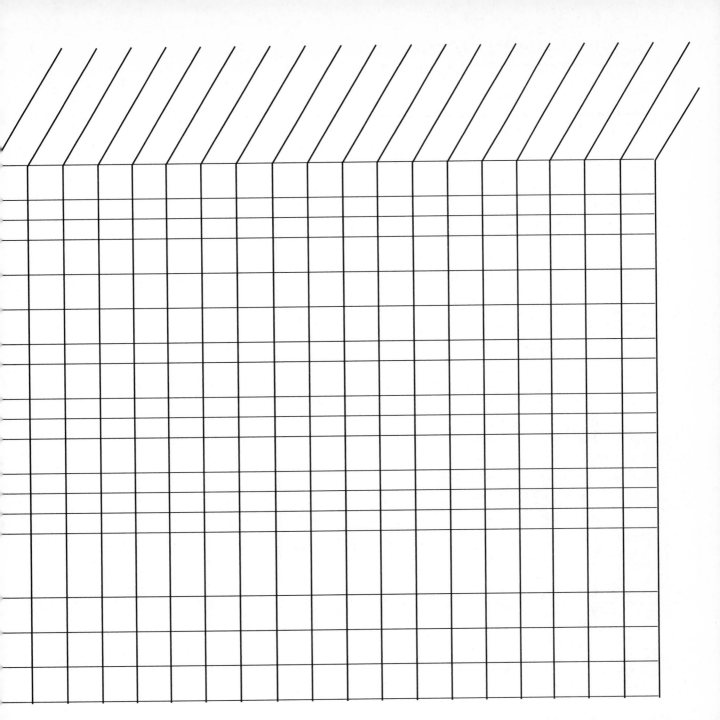

STUDENT PROGRESS PROFILE

CHILD'S NAME _____ YEAR _____ TEACHER _____

FOCUS	TOOL TITLE	PERFORMANCE LEVEL (Fill in letter code from key below.)			
		1st Assessment	2nd Assessment	3rd Assessment	4th Assessment

Performance Level Key

Related skills appear to be: **N = not yet apparent**   **B = beginning to develop**   **D = developing**
P = present   E = exceeding age expectations

WHOLE CLASS PROFILE

YEAR _____ TEACHER _____

FOCUS	TOOL TITLE										

Performance Level Key

Related skills appear to be: **N = not yet apparent   B = beginning to develop   D = developing**

P = present   E = exceeding age expectations

Assessment Planning Calendar

TEACHER _____

YEAR _____

AUGUST

_____
_____
_____
_____
_____
_____
_____
_____

SEPTEMBER

_____
_____
_____
_____
_____
_____
_____
_____

OCTOBER

_____
_____
_____
_____
_____
_____
_____
_____

NOVEMBER

_____
_____
_____
_____
_____
_____
_____
_____

Assessment Planning Calendar

TEACHER _____

YEAR _____

DECEMBER

_____
_____
_____
_____
_____
_____
_____
_____
_____

JANUARY

_____
_____
_____
_____
_____
_____
_____
_____
_____

FEBRUARY

_____
_____
_____
_____
_____
_____
_____
_____
_____

MARCH

_____
_____
_____
_____
_____
_____
_____
_____
_____

Assessment Planning Calendar

TEACHER _____

YEAR _____

APRIL

_____
_____
_____
_____
_____
_____
_____
_____
_____

MAY

_____
_____
_____
_____
_____
_____
_____
_____
_____

JUNE

_____
_____
_____
_____
_____
_____
_____
_____
_____

NOTES

_____
_____
_____
_____
_____
_____
_____
_____
_____

Appendix

TRY THIS!

Help your child learn about the concept of money. The next time you examine pocket change together, try this!

- Look at the fronts and backs of all the coins. Then play a game of heads and tails with one of the coins, making predictions about how many times the coin will land heads-up versus tails.
- Encourage your child to use vocabulary related to coins (e.g., penny, nickel, dime).
- Let your child earn a small allowance of change for jobs like picking up toys and save it for a purchase at a dollar store. Take opportunities to count money with your child and invite him or her to match coins.

MATHEMATICS: MEASUREMENT, TIME, AND MONEY

Partners in Learning

Dear Family and Caregivers,

Your child is studying important skills and concepts, including:

✪ _____

✪ _____

✪ _____

Please read the attached card that describes learning activities you can do at home with your child. These are suggested activities that take little time and yet truly support the work we're doing at school.

Together we can help every child improve his or her learning.

Sincerely,

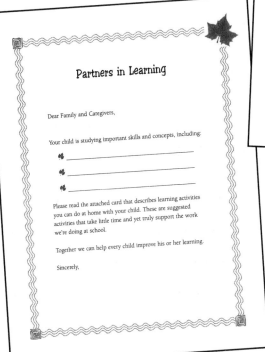

Partners in Learning

Dear Family and Caregivers,

Your child is studying important skills and concepts, including:

❧ _____

❧ _____

❧ _____

Please read the attached card that describes learning activities you can do at home with your child. These are suggested activities that take little time and yet truly support the work we're doing at school.

Together we can help every child improve his or her learning.

Sincerely,

TRY THIS!

Help your child learn about printing numerals and alphabet letters. The next time you write together, try this!

- Check your child's pencil grip for correctness. He or she should pinch the pencil with the thumb and index finger. (See illustration.)
- Hold your hand over your child's hand to guide and support writing movements.
- Write large numerals and letters that your child can trace with his or her fingers. Then try tracing a letter on your child's back and ask him or her to guess which letter it is.
- Draw a line on a sheet of paper and show your child how letters can be tall or short and how some letters hang down below the line.

LANGUAGE ARTS: WRITING

Partners in Learning

Dear Family and Caregivers,

Your child is studying important skills and concepts, including:

❧ _____

❧ _____

❧ _____

Please read the attached card that describes learning activities you can do at home with your child. These are suggested activities that take little time and yet truly support the work we're doing at school.

Together we can help every child improve his or her learning.

Sincerely,

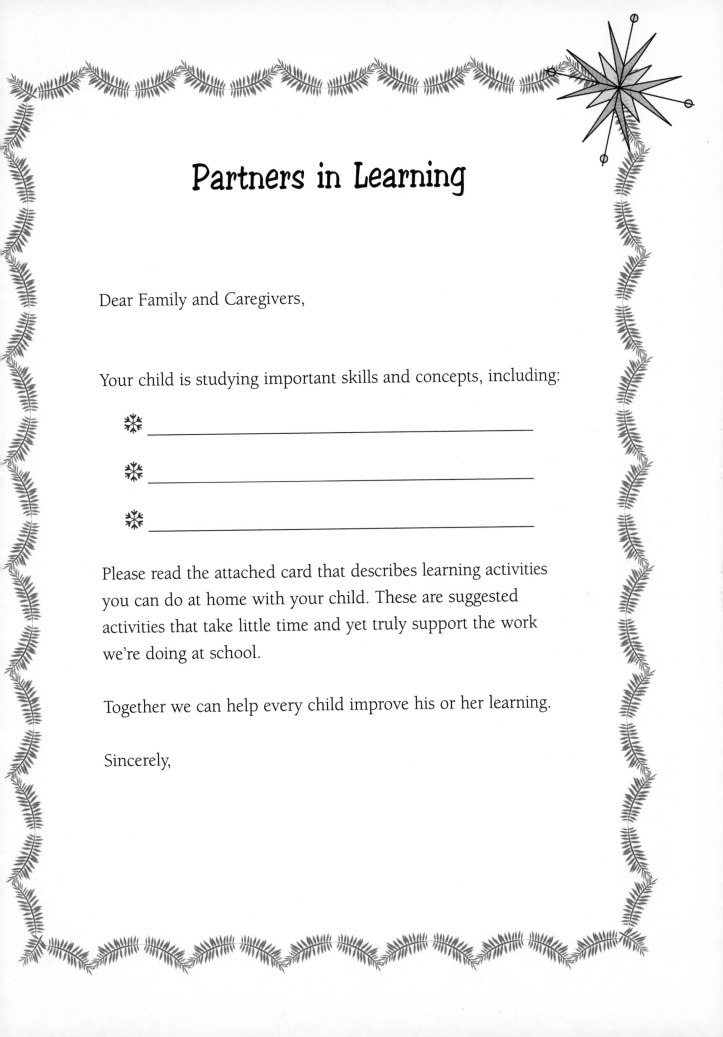

Partners in Learning

Dear Family and Caregivers,

Your child is studying important skills and concepts, including:

❄ _____

❄ _____

❄ _____

Please read the attached card that describes learning activities you can do at home with your child. These are suggested activities that take little time and yet truly support the work we're doing at school.

Together we can help every child improve his or her learning.

Sincerely,

Partners in Learning

Dear Family and Caregivers,

Your child is studying important skills and concepts, including:

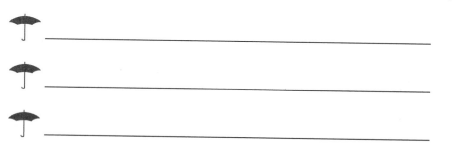

_____

_____

_____

Please read the attached card that describes learning activities you can do at home with your child. These are suggested activities that take little time and yet truly support the work we're doing at school.

Together we can help every child improve his or her learning.

Sincerely,

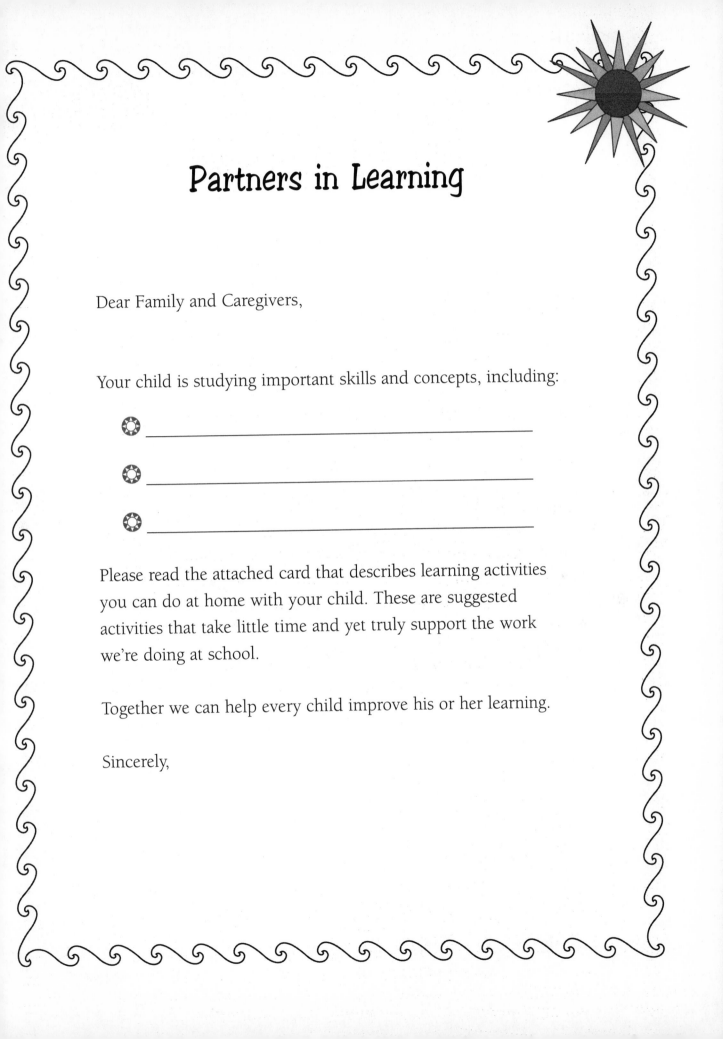

Partners in Learning

Dear Family and Caregivers,

Your child is studying important skills and concepts, including:

* _____

* _____

* _____

Please read the attached card that describes learning activities you can do at home with your child. These are suggested activities that take little time and yet truly support the work we're doing at school.

Together we can help every child improve his or her learning.

Sincerely,

TRY THIS!

Help your child learn about books and book handling. The next time you share a story together, try this!

- Examine the front cover, back cover, title page, and the title of the story.

- Track text while you read. Point at each word while you read it.

- Show how you read each page, following text from the top to the bottom of the page and left to right across the page. Show how you follow each line of text, making a return sweep down and left to pick up the next line to read.

- Discuss what a reader does when he or she sees different punctuation marks.

- Point to the page where the story begins and draw attention to the page where the story ends.

LANGUAGE ARTS: PRINT CONCEPTS

TRY THIS!

Help your child learn about the differences and similarities among words and sounds. The next time you play outdoors together, try this!

- Listen to and identify the sounds in your neighborhood (e.g., car horns, dogs barking, wind chimes).

- Play a variation of the game "hide and seek." Instead of having your child find you visually, ask him or her to locate you by isolating the sounds you make. (Enclosed play spaces and parks work best for this activity.)

- Make a comical game out of listening to the differences between words that sound similar (e.g., stop and hop, run and ran, stump and jump).

LANGUAGE ARTS: AUDITORY DISCRIMINATION

TRY THIS!

Help your child learn about differences and similarities among words and sounds. The next time you feel silly together, try this!

- Tune in the radio and sing along to music, improvise instrumental sounds, and tap or clap to the rhythm.

- Read stories that play with language and sounds. Roar like a lion. Squeak like a mouse. Have fun recreating sounds and nonsense words.

- Play listening games like inviting your child to repeat the beats of a pattern that you clap.

LANGUAGE ARTS: AUDITORY DISCRIMINATION

TRY THIS!

Help your child notice differences and similarities between objects. The next time you're in the kitchen together, try this!

- Sort a collection of objects to see how items are the same and different. (Spoons, storage containers, and potatoes work well for this activity.)

- Examine alphabet letters. Observe and compare attributes like tallness, shortness, curves, straight lines, and angles. (Magnetic letters that stick on a refrigerator work well for this activity.)

- Put away clean objects from the drying rack or dishwasher. Talk together about the sorting process. (Plastic storage containers, sturdy dishes, and bladeless utensils are safest for this activity.)

LANGUAGE ARTS: VISUAL DISCRIMINATION

TRY THIS!

Help your child learn about rhyming words. The next time you ride or drive somewhere together, try this!

- Sing songs with words that rhyme. Make up your own verses.

- Repeat nursery rhymes. Wait for your child to fill in the missing words. (e.g., "Jack and Jill went up the _____"). Make it a game!

- Read-aloud books with wonderful rhymes. (Dr. Seuss books are great examples of word play books.) Invite your child to listen as you read a page and then identify words in the story that rhyme.

LANGUAGE ARTS: PHONOLOGICAL AWARENESS

TRY THIS!

Help your child notice individual sounds within words and individual words within sentences. The next time you ride or drive somewhere together, try this!

- Tell your child to clap or tap once for every beat in a word you say. You might begin with short words and move on to longer words. For example: *dog* (one clap), *breakfast* (two claps), *hippopotamus* (five claps).

- Count and discuss how many words you hear in everyday sentences. You might begin with short sentences and move on to longer sentences. For example: *Look out!* (2), *Where are we now?* (4), *I see the soccer field.* (5).

LANGUAGE ARTS: PHONOLOGICAL AWARENESS

TRY THIS!

Help your child learn about identifying and deleting parts of compound words. The next time you walk, ride, or drive somewhere together, try this!

- Ask your child to solve a riddle by building a compound word. You might say, "A storm with thunder is a . . . ?" (*thunderstorm*)

- Talk about words that are made up of two smaller words. Explain that the first word describes the second word (e.g., *mailbox*). Here are some more words to get you started: *beanbag, bedtime, doghouse, fishbowl, football, paintbrush, playground, postcard, sandbox, spaceship, toothbrush*, and *washcloth*.

LANGUAGE ARTS: PHONOLOGICAL AWARENESS

TRY THIS!

Help your child learn to identify the beginning, middle, and ending sounds in words. The next time you walk, ride, or drive somewhere together, try this!

- Play a listening game. Tell your child that you will ask which word in a pair has a specific sound. Then explain that your child should listen to find out the position of that sound. The sound may fall at the beginning, middle, or end.
  You might say, "Which word has the /n/ sound at its beginning . . . *mom* or *never?*" (never) Repeat the process with other sounds and words. Here are some sounds and word pairs to get you started:

Beginning Sound: /a/   apple, dog (apple)
Middle Sound: /l/   band, silly (silly)
Ending Sound: /p/   cap, rub (cap)

LANGUAGE ARTS: PHONEMIC AWARENESS

TRY THIS!

Help your child learn how to differentiate between sounds in oral language. The next time you learn together, try this!

- Encourage your child to listen carefully to hear specific sounds in a word. Say, "Do you hear a /p/ at the beginning of the word *pig*? Do you hear a /g/ at the end of the word *car*? Where is the /a/ in *dad*?"

- Play 'I spy' to learn about beginning and ending sounds. Select an object in the room and give a hint with the beginning or ending sound (e.g., for a ball, say, "I spy something that starts with /b/"). Invite your child guess the word.

- Have your child pick from a deck of alphabet letter cards and find something in the room that has the same beginning, middle, or ending sound as the sound you read from the card. Ask your child to repeat the sound as he or she hunts for the object.

LANGUAGE ARTS: PHONEMIC AWARENESS

TRY THIS!

Help your child learn how to blend and segment the sounds in a word. The next time you play together, try this!

- Encourage your child to "push together" the sounds you make to discover a word. Say, "Listen, what's my word? /d/-/o/-/g/." Assist your child, if necessary to blend the sounds together to make *dog*—the way he or she will do when first reading. To segment the sounds for writing words, ask your child to separate the sounds of a word. Say, "Let's sound out the word *dog* . . . *dog* . . . /d/-/o/-/g/." Repeat with simple words until the child is ready for more challenging ones.

- Bounce a ball for each sound your child hears in a word. For the word *it*, for instance, he or she would bounce the ball twice—once for /i/ and once for /t/.

LANGUAGE ARTS: PHONEMIC AWARENESS

TRY THIS!

Help your child learn how to substitute one sound for another. The next time you unwind together, try this!

- Sing songs that require modifying the beginning sounds in words (e.g., *Bingo*).

- Read and repeat nursery rhymes and verses.

- Change the rhyming words in favorite nursery rhymes (e.g., Jack fell down and broke his *frown*.).

- Brainstorm lists of rhyming words. Talk about why the words rhyme. Change the beginning sound to make up nonsense words.

- Read stories with playful language.

LANGUAGE ARTS: PHONEMIC AWARENESS

TRY THIS!

Help your child develop his or her reading fluency. The next time you read together, try this!

- Read a line of text and then ask your child to repeat it (like an echo).

- Discuss what a reader does when he or she sees different punctuation marks.

- Encourage your child to read with expression.

- Think aloud about what you're reading and how you're reading favorite recipes, magazines, newspapers, and so on.

- Tape record yourself reading a short story aloud. Invite your child to read along with your taped voice. Then, have your child record and share a story he or she has practiced reading.

LANGUAGE ARTS: READING

TRY THIS!

Help your child learn the value of reading. The next time you share a book together, try this!

- Read aloud expressively with your child.

- Practice saying letter sounds and blending sounds together in order to identify words.

- Talk about the illustrations (e.g., how they enrich the story or explain the text).

- Invite your child to make predictions about what will happen next or how the story will end.

LANGUAGE ARTS: READING

TRY THIS!

Help your child learn about reading for enjoyment. The next time you share a book together, try this!

- Explain how different text formats meet different purposes. Examine newspapers, postcards, recipes, and so on.

- Discuss favorite words, characters, scenes, and plot twists.

- Read together for at least fifteen minutes.

- Share a treasured story over and over again.

LANGUAGE ARTS: READING

TRY THIS!

Help your child develop fine motor skills for writing. The next time you unwind together, try this!

- Have your child use safety scissors to cut out shapes and make crafts.

- Encourage your child to paint or draw using a vertical or inclined surface (e.g., easel).

- Toss and catch a beanbag or small ball.

- Pop plastic packing wrap or sculpt with play dough.

- Play with toys and games that require your child to use small muscles (for grasping, constructing, and sorting).

LANGUAGE ARTS: WRITING

TRY THIS!

Help your child learn about printing numerals and alphabet letters. The next time you write together, try this!

- Check your child's pencil grip for correctness. He or she should pinch the pencil with the thumb and index finger. (See illustration.)

- Hold your hand over your child's hand to guide and support writing movements.

- Write large numerals and letters that your child can trace with his or her fingers. Then try tracing a letter on your child's back and ask him or her to guess which letter it is.

- Draw a line on a sheet of paper and show your child how letters can be tall or short and how some letters hang down below the line.

LANGUAGE ARTS: WRITING

TRY THIS!

Help your child spot differences and similarities between forms. The next time you study shapes together, try this!

- Create a game out of spotting shapes. Say the name of a shape and invite your child to find a few objects in the room or outside with the same shape. Have your child point out curves, straight edges, sharp angles, and so on.

- Draw simple shapes (e.g., circles, squares, triangles). Invite your child to trace each shape with his or her finger and then draw the shapes with a pencil or crayon.

MATHEMATICS: SHAPES

TRY THIS!

Help your child learn how we use numbers every day. The next time you talk about them together, try this!

- Draw attention to numerals related to prices, times, ingredient lists, television channels, and so on.

- Use a calendar to count and mark the days until a special event (e.g., birthday).

- Encourage your child to recite your phone number and street address.

MATHEMATICS: NUMERATION

TRY THIS!

Help your child learn about the link between quantities and numerals. The next time you have fun together, try this!

- Play games that involve cards, dice, or dominoes.
- Count how many people are playing a board game and then give one snack or treat to each person.
- Measure your child's height on a growth chart. Read the numerals to tell how tall he or she is. Weigh your child. Read the numerals to tell how much he or she weighs.

MATHEMATICS: NUMERATION

TRY THIS!

Help your child learn how to compare sets by number. The next time you organize a closet or shelves together, try this!

- Sort and count favorite belongings (e.g., books, marbles, trains).
- Gather and count collections from nature (e.g., pinecones, rocks, seashells).
- Count out sets of a particular number. (e.g., "Please get me three clean shirts.").

MATHEMATICS: NUMERATION/ORDERING AND SORTING

TRY THIS!

Help your child learn about ordering and sorting. The next time you do the laundry together, try this!

- Talk about the process. Discuss what laundry tasks need to be done first, second, and so on.
- Gather clothes to wash and sort them by color.
- Sort clean socks by attributes such as size, color, and pattern. Have your child put like pairs together.

MATHEMATICS: ORDERING AND SORTING

TRY THIS!

Help your child learn about patterns. The next time you play together, try this!

- Look for patterns in nature (e.g., flowers, tree rings, turtle shells).
- Identify patterns made by man (e.g., ceramic tiles, decorative windows, garden gates).
- Make patterns with found items such as coins and buttons. Ask your child to match your pattern, extend your pattern, and make a pattern of his or her own.

MATHEMATICS: ORDERING AND SORTING

TRY THIS!

Help your child learn about length, weight, and capacity. The next time you go grocery shopping together, try this!

- Draw attention to how foods are packaged and priced. You might point out that two boxes of frozen pops cost the same, but that one box has twelve pops while the other has just eight.

- Weigh bags of fruits and vegetables on the produce department's scales and discuss the results.

MATHEMATICS: MEASUREMENT, TIME, AND MONEY

TRY THIS!

Help your child learn about the concepts of time and money. The next time you go grocery shopping together, try this!

- Think aloud as you select ingredients for a favorite recipe. Discuss how you can estimate how much of an item you need and how much time the recipe will take to prepare.

- Talk about paper money and coins. Invite your child to count the pennies you receive in your change.

MATHEMATICS: MEASUREMENT, TIME, AND MONEY

TRY THIS!

Help your child learn about measuring tools. The next time you ride or drive somewhere together, try this!

- Listen to the weather forecast on the radio. Talk about what tool a meteorologist uses to determine temperature (thermometer). Then help your child think of other occasions for using a thermometer.

- Estimate how long you think it will take to travel to your destination and return home. Then use a watch to time how long it actually takes.

- Discuss how we can record distance. Identify different standard units of measure (e.g., inches, yards, miles).

MATHEMATICS: MEASUREMENT, TIME, AND MONEY

TRY THIS!

Help your child learn about the concept of money. The next time you examine pocket change together, try this!

- Look at the fronts and backs of all the coins. Then play a game of heads and tails with one of the coins, making predictions about how many times the coin will land heads-up versus tails.

- Encourage your child to use vocabulary related to coins (e.g., penny, nickel, dime).

- Let your child earn a small allowance of change for jobs like picking up toys and save it for a purchase at a dollar store. Take opportunities to count the money with your child and invite him or her to match coins.

MATHEMATICS: MEASUREMENT, TIME, AND MONEY

TRY THIS!

Help your child learn about the concept of time. The next time your child asks what time it is, try this!

- Talk about a good time you shared recently. Ask specific questions about the sequence of events (e.g., "Who arrived at the field first?" "What did we do after that?").

- Encourage your child to use vocabulary that relates to the concept of time (e.g., *before, now, tomorrow*) and the measurement of time (*seconds, minutes, hours*).

- Brainstorm tools and methods for measuring time (e.g., kitchen timers, hourglasses, calendars).

MATHEMATICS: MEASUREMENT, TIME, AND MONEY

TRY THIS!

Help your child explore geometry. The next time you play together, try this!

- Stack, roll, and slide three-dimensional shapes. (Blocks, cans, and balls work well for this activity.)

- Draw attention to objects that look different when they are turned sideways or flipped over (e.g., cones, canisters, prisms).

- Encourage your child to use mathematical language—including words that describe spatial relationships (e.g., *above, near, under*) and words that name geometric solids (e.g., *sphere, cube, cylinder*).

MATHEMATICS: SPATIAL RELATIONSHIPS AND TERMINOLOGY

TRY THIS!

Help your child practice addition and subtraction skills. The next time you share a meal together, try this!

- Ask your child to solve addition sentences. For example, over dinner say, "You have two carrots on your plate. If I give you two more, how many carrots will you have altogether?"

- Invite your child to solve subtraction sentences. Try this, "There were six cookies on that dish. Ezra ate one. How many cookies are there now?"

- Have your child count how many people will be sitting at the table. Work together to set a place setting for each person.

MATHEMATICS: OPERATION AND PLACE VALUE/NUMERATION

TRY THIS!

Help your child learn to organize data. The next time you're stuck inside on a rainy day, try this!

- Create a simple map with your child to show the route you take from his or her bed to the nearest fire escape. Talk about turning left and right.

- Use a calendar at home. Mark off special days. Predict how many days until the next event. Talk about how the information is organized on a grid or boxes on the calendar. Use the calendar as you discuss things that have happened and that will happen, referring to *yesterday*, *today*, and *tomorrow*.

MATHEMATICS: DATA MANAGEMENT

TRY THIS!

Help your child learn about collecting and organizing information. The next time you go shopping together, try this!

• Tell your child to make a list of a few favorite ice cream flavors. Ask other family members to choose one of those flavors as a favorite.

As family members share information, help your child organize and tally the results. Then work together to represent those results with a graph. (Bar graphs and pictographs, or picture graphs, are ideal formats for this activity.)

MATHEMATICS: CHARTS AND GRAPHS

TRY THIS!

Help your child learn about charts and graphs. The next time you unpack the groceries together, try this!

• Examine graphs and charts printed on product packaging. Try to find one example of a circle (or pie) chart, bar graph, and pictograph. Talk about how charts and graphs present information.

• Look for the Food Guide Pyramid symbol. Or, read about it online at the United States Department of Agriculture's *MyPyramid.gov*. Discuss ways the chart can help your child make nutritious choices about food.

MATHEMATICS: CHARTS AND GRAPHS

Your Child's First Report Card

When a child starts elementary school, parents may feel anxious and excited about how their child is doing in school and how to support his or her learning. If your child attended preschool, a report card is similar to a progress report your child may have received. For children who did not attend preschool, this might be the first time parents will receive a report on your child's progress. Progress reports and report cards are great opportunities to learn about your child's strengths and identify any areas he may need help with. They can serve as a way to continue communicating with your child's teacher and to share your own observations about your child's skills and interests. The National Association for the Education of Young Children (NAEYC) offers suggestions for parents and caregivers to prepare for this benchmark in school.

Take time for ongoing discussions with both your child and his teacher about what is going on in class. Ideally, you know how your child is doing in school, and report cards serve as a periodic review of progress.

❖ Talk with your child each day about class assignments, what he or she did, and what he or she learned.

❖ Communicate with your child's teacher on a regular basis. This might be done through a phone call or e-mail. Some teachers provide informal feedback between report cards, such as a portfolio of a child's schoolwork.

❖ Share with your child the information you receive from the teacher throughout the year. Talk about the things he or she does well and those skills he or she is just beginning to develop.

❖ Offer specific praise and encouragement on your child's work. This will help your child recognize the skills that he or she has, build a sense of confidence, and motivate him or her to continue focusing on schoolwork.

Know when report cards come out and prepare with your child. Remember, your child may not know what report cards are or why he or she is getting one.

❖ Discuss the purpose of the report card and what the grades or comments mean.

❖ Encourage your child to tell you how he or she thinks school is going at all times, and especially before the report card comes.

❖ Talk with your child about developing skills. Point out what he or she can do already and things he or she is just learning.

❖ Use the information to acknowledge strengths and areas where you and her teacher will help her to improve.

Take an active role in your child's school all year around.

❖ Get to know your child's teacher; attend parent-teacher conferences and other school-sponsored parent activities.

❖ Ask the teacher what criteria are used to determine children's progress—class participation, tests, homework assignments, portfolios, or other methods. Ask to see this information between report cards.

❖ Check the school calendar for report card dates and other school events.

❖ Contact the teacher whenever you don't understand grades or policies.

Invest time in your child's education outside school.

❖ Foster his or her interest in learning through educational experiences that allow your child to gain hands-on learning in topics that interest him or her.

❖ Read to and with your child every day.

❖ Limit time spent watching television or playing video and computer games.

❖ Establish a family routine. This includes time for homework and studying, as well as eating meals, doing chores, playing with friends, and going to bed at a set time.

Use these tips at report card times and throughout the year to track your child's progress and seek help as needed. Stay involved in your child's education and help her succeed in school! Early Years Are Learning Years is a regular series from NAEYC providing families with tips for giving their young children a great start on learning.

Raising a Reader

Children learn to love the sound of language before they ever notice the existence of printed words on a page. They coo or babble when you talk or sing to them, and as they grow, rapidly pick up the concepts and words they hear used. Reading aloud with children is an essential component to language development and is one of the most important activities for preparing them to succeed as readers.

As parents and caregivers, you can help lay down the foundation for a love of reading and nurture children's development. Here are some things you can do to raise a lifelong reader:

TALK, SING, AND PLAY

Young children delight in hearing language. Talk as you do simple everyday things together: recite nursery rhymes, and do finger plays, games, and action songs.

MAKE TIME TO READ

Try to read with your child every day at a regularly scheduled time. If possible, choose a time when you can be relaxed and not rushed. If you have more than one child, spend time reading with each child separately, especially if they're more than two years apart. On days that are particularly hectic, bring a few books when you take children along on errands. Taking time to read to children on a regular basis sends the message that reading is worthwhile.

ONE MORE TIME . . . PLEASE?!

As every adult who cares for children knows, they often ask to hear the same story again and again. They delight in knowing what comes next and often learn a favorite book so well that they can "read" it on their own. That favorite story may speak to your child's current interests and emotional needs, so it's important for the adults in their lives to be patient during this phase. Young children are eventually ready for different stories if they are continually exposed to a variety of books.

SLOW DOWN

It's not just what you read to children, but how you read that matters. If adults rush through stories or read without enthusiasm, children quickly lose interest. Try to read with expression and use different voices for the characters. Reading at a leisurely pace with occasional pauses gives children time to take in what they hear, mull it over, and imagine the people, places, and events. Pose a question or make a remark that will prompt the child to think, express himself, or relate the story to his or her own experiences. It's also a good idea to follow children's cues. Sometimes they are caught up in the story and don't want stops and detours along the way.

CHOOSE BOOKS WITH CARE

Reading together often, you learn a lot about the kinds of books your child likes and understands. Visit the local library and involve your child in deciding what to bring home. Selecting books that relate to what's happening in the child's life at that time is a good way to ease transitions and allay fears about upcoming events. Topics such as new siblings, adoption, or moving to a new home are covered in a variety of books that are written specifically for young children.

SURROUND CHILDREN WITH READING MATERIAL

In addition to library books, children also like having some books of their own that they can read whenever the mood strikes them. Affordable used books can be found at yard sales, thrift stores, secondhand bookstores, and public library book sales. Consider subscribing to a good children's magazine—children love having something come in the mail just for them!

DON'T PRESSURE CHILDREN ABOUT WHAT OR WHEN TO READ

Nagging children about their reading habits may cause them to resist reading all together. Some school-age children choose to read only comic books or fan magazines after their homework is completed. Try not to criticize—after all, they are reading. If a child makes a mistake when reading aloud, don't interrupt. If the mistake doesn't change the meaning, let it go.

SHOW THAT YOU VALUE THEIR EFFORTS

Nothing is more important for fostering readers than showing genuine enthusiasm. Ask your child to read to you, a younger child, or a special visitor. Talk with him or her about what he or she is reading and respond positively.

Mathematics Through Play

Everyday routines and play events offer rich opportunities for teaching your children about mathematics. Integrating math into all parts of the day multiplies the learning and gives young children an understanding that math is part of everyday life.

During the early years of life, children play with concepts of size, number, shape, and quantity. They discover that objects exist, can be moved, and can be fitted together. As they acquire language, children begin to make statements indicating their knowledge of mathematical concepts. Their play and language form the basis for learning about math in natural ways, and one great way to integrate math involves hands-on activities and problem-solving situations that pique your children's curiosity.

AT THE KITCHEN COUNTER

Try constructing a math puzzle with three empty glasses. In the first glass, pour the milk up to the brim. Fill the second glass halfway, and leave the third glass empty. Then ask your children to identify which glass is empty, which is full, and which is one-half full. Most preschool-age children will understand the meaning of full, and will be able to identify the full glass of milk. Many young children will also understand the concepts of empty and more, but may have trouble with half and less.

IN THE GROCERY STORE

Explore these same concepts through a grocery shopping game. Give your children plastic cups and containers of dried beans. Ask them to take three cups and to fill one cup full of beans, leave one cup empty, and fill the third cup with fewer beans than the full cup but more than the empty one. Through these repeated interactions and dialogue, young children can learn some of the vocabulary and concepts that underlie mathematics such as equations, fractions, and the notion of zero.

IN THE LIVING ROOM

Measuring tapes or other measuring tools, whether in standard or nonstandard units, create enjoyable learning activities. For example, your children can use safe, household tools to measure blocks. Or, they may measure blocks using smaller blocks and then compare the results to see which block is longer or which is thicker.

Ready for a read aloud? Math concepts make an appearance in many children's books, such as *One, Two, Three!* by Sandra Boynton, *The Very Hungry Caterpillar* by Eric Carle, and *Measuring Penny* by Loreen Leedy. Visit your local library to access a treasure trove of books that support math learning.

Young children who learn number concepts and other mathematical knowledge through hands-on play activities and discussions gain a broad understanding of math skills. When you think of activities for your children, focus not just on having fun but also on creating a learning environment that stimulates and nurtures their inquisitive minds. These daily routines and play activities can give them a great start on thinking about and using mathematics.

Adapted from "Integrating Mathematicians for Young Children Through Play" by Smita Guha, an article in the NAEYC journal, *Young Children*.

Singing as a Teaching Tool

It doesn't take an experienced musician to sing with young children. Anyone can sing "Row, Row, Row Your Boat," and make the motions of rowing a boat. Parents and teachers can lead many singing and musical games, even if they consider themselves nonmusical.

Music is a great way to engage young children because it is a natural and enjoyable part of their everyday lives. Children hear music or sing while watching television, riding in the car, at school, and as part of bedtime rituals. We often hear children creating their own songs and incorporating music in their play. Music is a socially engaging way to learn, and especially appropriate for the developmental levels of young children.

The concept of using music to teach is not new. Many young children learn to recite the alphabet by singing the ABCs, and educational television programs for young children, such as Sesame Street, use a lot of music in their programming. Researchers have found that music can help children learn multiplication tables and improve early literacy skills. Many adults still remember lessons connected to music from their childhood.

Music helps many children break information down into easily remembered pieces or associate it with previously known information, such as a familiar song. One study found that using familiar melodies helped five-year-olds learn phone numbers at a faster rate than using no music or unfamiliar melodies.

Singing with children can be an especially fun and valuable experience. When you sing with young children, you can adjust the speed and volume to fit their abilities. You don't need to sound like a professional singer. As long as you are enthusiastic, young children will enjoy it, and want to sing along.

You can also pair singing with movement or visual aids that stimulate the senses. This allows children to not only hear the music, but also feel and move to the rhythms, and see, touch, and play the instruments.

Singing also gives you lots of opportunities to teach new words to young children. By taking familiar songs (such as "Twinkle, Twinkle, Little Star," "Frère Jacques/Are You Sleeping?" "Three Blind Mice" or other songs from your childhood) and changing or adding words, you can introduce new vocabulary in a way that makes it easy for children to follow along.

You can create individualized songs that will engage children and boost their memories. Fill your songs with people (for example, family members, teachers or friends), objects (clothing, furniture, cars or bikes), daily rituals (brushing teeth, bedtime), and special events (holidays, going on a field trip) that are an important part of children's lives.

While music is a great way to introduce new words, it can also contribute to children's progress and learning in many different areas. Music supports self-expression, cooperative play, creativity, emotional well being, and development of social, cognitive, communication, and motor skills. Music and singing are fun and effective ways to help young children learn.

Adapted from "Music as a Teaching Tool: Creating Story Songs" by Shelly Ringgenberg, an article in the NAEYC journal, *Young Children*.

WORD FAMILY ENDINGS

Words that share the same ending sound (rime) *and* share the same spelling of that sound are often said to be in the same word family. Here is a list of word family endings you can use for a quick reference.

-ab	-ate	-ig	_____
-ace	-aw	-ill	-ub
-ack	-ay	-im	-ud
-ad	_____	-in	-uff
-ag	-eck	-ing	-um
-all	-ed	-ink	-un
-am	-ell	-ip	-ush
-ame	-em	-ish	-ut
-an	-en	-it	
-and	-end	_____	
-ang	-ent	-ob	
-ank	-est	-ock	
-ap	-et	-od	
-ape	_____	-og	
-ar	-ice	-old	
-are	-ick	-ong	
-ash	-id	-ook	
-at	-ide	-op	
	-iff	-ot	

THE REST OF THE CODE: DIGRAPHS

While there are only 26 letters of the alphabet, there are more than 40 sounds in the English language. Many of these sounds are represented by digraphs, combinations of two letters that create a single sound (e.g., *ng*, *sh*, *ar*). Pre-kindergarten children should be introduced to digraphs and the letters that represent them through oral language and synthetic phonics activities. This chart provides the 'rest of the code' for reading and writing words that have the regular spelling of digraphs (e.g., *coat*, *wait*, *meet*, *then*, *chip*).

oa goat	**ie** pie	**ai** rain	**ee** week
ue cue	**sh** ship	**ch** chin	**th** thing
ng sing	**or** for	**oo** book	**oo** coo
ou ouch	**oi** boil	**er** her	**ar** car

References

BOOKS AND ARTICLES

Abrohms, A. (1992). *Mathematical discoveries for young children: Using manipulatives.* Lincolnshire, Illinois: Learning Resources, Inc.

Adams, M. J. (1998). *Phonemic awareness in young children.* Baltimore, Maryland; Paul H. Brookes Publishing.

Moats, L. C. (1999). *Teaching reading is rocket science: What expert teachers of reading should know and be able to do.* Washington, DC: American Federation of Teachers.

American Federation of Teachers. (1999). *Building on the best, learning from what works: Five promising remedial reading intervention programs.* Washington, DC. American Federation of Teachers.

Booth, D. (1996). *Literacy techniques for building successful readers and writers.* York, Maine: Stenhouse Publishers.

Carson-Dellosa's Hands-on science: Preschool-kindergarten. (1991). Greensboro, NC. Carson-Dellosa Publishing Co., Inc.

Clay, M. M. (1993). *An observation survey of early literacy achievement.* Portsmouth, NH: Heinemann.

Clay, M. M. (1991). *Becoming literate: The construction of inner control.* Portsmouth, NH: Heinemann.

Clay, M. M. (1993). *Reading recovery: A guidebook for teachers in training.* Portsmouth, NH: Heinemann.

Cunningham, P. M. & Allington, R. L. (1998). *Classrooms that work: They can all read and write.* 2nd ed. New York, NY: Addison, Wesley Longman.

Daniels, H. (1996). *Literature circles.* Portsmouth, NH: Heinemann.

Dupree, H. & Iversen, S. (1994). *Early literacy in the classroom: A new standard for young readers.* Ellerslie, Auckland, New Zealand: Lands End Publishing.

Fitzpatrick, J. (1997). *Phonemic awareness.* Huntington Beach, CA: Creative Teaching Press, Inc.

Fitzpatrick, J. (1999). *Teaching beginning writing.* Huntington Beach, CA: Creative Teaching Press, Inc.

Fountas, I. & Pinnell, G. S. (1996). *Guided reading.* Portsmouth, NH: Heinemann.

Fountas, I. & Pinnell, G. S. (1998). *Word matters.* Portsmouth, NH: Heinemann.

Fountas, I. & Pinnell, G. S. (Eds.). (1998). *Voices on word matters: Learning about phonics and spelling in the literacy classroom.* Portsmouth, NH: Heinemann.

Gaskins, I., et al. (December 1996/ January 1997). Procedures for word learning: Making discoveries about words. *The Reading Teacher.* Vol 50. No. 4.

Gilbert, L. (1989). *Do touch: Instant, easy hands-on learning experiences for young children.* Mt. Rainer, Maryland: Gryphon House.

Hall, D. P. & Cunningham. P. M. (1998). *Month-by-month reading and writing for kindergarten.* Greensboro, NC: Carson-Dellosa.

Hall, D. P. & Williams, E. (2000). *The teacher's guide to the building blocks.* Greensboro, NC: Carson-Dellosa.

Healy, J. M. (1994) *Your child's growing mind: A practical guide to brain development and learning from birth to adolescence.* Revised Edition. New York, NY: Doubleday.

Jordano, K. & Callella-Jones, T. (1998). *Phonemic awareness songs and rhymes for fall (winter & summer).* Huntington Beach, CA: Creative Teaching Press, Inc.

Kepler, L. (1996). *A year of hands-on science.* New York, NY: Scholastic.

Lloyd, Sue. (1993). *The phonics handbook.* (Jolly Phonics). Essex, United Kingdom: Jolly Learning Company.

Love, E. & Reilly, S. (1996). *A sound way: phonics activities for early literacy.* Markham, ON, Canada: Pembroke Publishers Ltd.

SchifferDanoff, V. (1995). *The Scholastic integrated language arts resource book.* New York, NY: Scholastic.

SchifferDanoff, V. (1996). *The pocket chart book.* New York, NY: Scholastic.

Schiller, P. & Peterson, L. (1997). *Count on math: activities for small hands and lively minds.* Beltsville, Maryland: Gryphon House.

Schlosser, K. & Phillips V. (1992). *Building literacy with interactive charts.* New York. NY: Scholastic.

Schwartz. S. & Bone, M. (1995). *Retelling, relating, reflecting: Beyond the 3 R's.* Toronto, ON, Canada: Irwin Publishing.

Sunflower, Cherlyn. (1993). *75 creative ways to publish students' writing.* New York, NY: Scholastic.

Taberski, S. (2000). *On solid ground: Strategies for teaching reading K–3.* Portsmouth NH: Heinemann.

INTERNET RESOURCES

Chard, D., Simmons, D., Kameenui, E. *Understanding the primary role of word recognition in the reading process: A synthesis of research on beginning reading.* University of Oregon.
http://idea.uoregon.edu/~ncite/documents/techrep/tech15.html

Collins, V., Dickson, S., Simmons, D., Kameenui, E. *Metacognition and its relation to reading comprehension: A synthesis of the research.* University of Oregon.
http://idea.uoregon.edu/~ncite/documents/techrep/tech23.html

Critical issues: Addressing the literacy needs of emergent and early readers. North Central regional Educational Laboratory (NCREL).
http://www.ncrel.org/sdrs/areas/issues/content/cntareas/reading/h100.htm

Grossen, B. (1997). *Synthesis of research on reading from the NICHD.*
http://www.nrrt.org/synthesis_research.htm

Gunn, B., Simmons, D., Kameenui, E. *Emergent literacy: Synthesis of the research.* University of Oregon.
http://idea.uoregon.edu/~ncite/documents/techrep/tech19.html

McREL Standards. (Mid-Continent Research for Education and Learning). Compendium of K–12 standards.
http://www.mcrel.org/standards-benchmarks

Ministry of Education and Training (1998). *The kindergarten program.* Toronto, ON: Queen's Printer for Ontario.
http://www.edu.gov.on.ca

Moore, P. (2000). *Early literacy intervention and the "reading wars": The bottom line on reading programs: Most work some of the time, with some students.* Center for Early Literacy Director, University of Maine.
http://www.ume.maine.edu/~cel/intvntn.htm

National Association for the Education of Young Children. NAEYC initial standards.
https://www.naeyc.org

National Council of Teachers of Mathematics (NCTM). Pre-K to grade 2 standards.
https://www.nctm.org

The National Reading Panel (2000). *Teaching children to read: An evidenced-based assessment of the scientific research literature on reading and its implication for reading instruction—reports of subgroups.*
http://www.nationalreadingpanel.org

Snow, C., Burns, S., Griffin, P. *Preventing reading difficulties in young children*. National Research Council.
http://zuni.nm.us/Ias/read/Prevent/ch4.htm

Smith, S., Simmons, D., Kameenui, E. *Synthesis of research on phonological awareness: Principles and implication for reading acquisition*. University of Oregon.
http://idea.uoregon.edu/~ncite/documents/techrep/tech21.html

Notes